THE ISLANDS SERIES

JERSEY

THE ISLANDS SERIES

†Achill
†The Åland Islands
†Alderney
†The Aran Islands
†The Isle of Arran
†The Island of Bute
*Canary Islands: Fuerteventura
*Cape Breton Island .
*Corsica
*Crete
*Cyprus
*Dominica
*The Falkland Islands
†Gotland
*Grand Bahama
*Greenland
†Harris and Lewis
†The Isle of Mull
†Lundy
†The Maltese Islands
*Mauritius
*Minorca
†Orkney
*Puerto Rico
*Rhodes
*The Ryukyu Islands
†St Kilda and Other Hebridean
   Islands
*Sardinia

†The Isles of Scilly
*The Seychelles
†Shetland
*Singapore
†Skye
*The Solomon Islands
†Staffa
*Tasmania
†Uists and Barra
*Vancouver Island

in preparation

Bermuda
Colonsay and Oronsay
Fiji
Guadeloupe
Guernsey
Inner Hebrides
Islay
Jamaica
St Helena
Sark
Tahiti
Tobago
Tonga
Valentia

* Published in the United States by Stackpole
† Published in the United States by David & Charles Inc
The series is distributed in Australia by Wren Publishing Pty Ltd, Melbourne

JERSEY

by *WARD RUTHERFORD*

DAVID & CHARLES

NEWTON ABBOT LONDON NORTH POMFRET (VT) VANCOUVER

ISBN 0 7153 7075 8
Library of Congress Catalog Card Number
75-31326

Set in 11 on 13pt Monotype Baskerville
and printed in Great Britain
by Latimer Trend & Company Ltd Plymouth
for David & Charles (Publishers) Limited
Brunel House Newton Abbot Devon

Published in the United States of America
by David & Charles Inc
North Pomfret Vermont 05053 USA

Published in Canada
by Douglas David & Charles Limited
1875 Welch Street North Vancouver BC

CONTENTS

5

ILLUSTRATIONS

7

ILLUSTRATIONS

MAPS

8

INTRODUCTION

JERSEY is compounded of three elements: sky, sea and granite. Every image is shot through with them. A canopy of sky—cloudless in summer, pouring down its brilliant light on trees, buildings, fields and cows which turn their slow and ruminant gaze on passers-by; or turbulent and grey in winter with the white gulls screaming and gliding upon it.

The sea, too, is many-coloured. Blue and sun-sparkling as glimpsed between the arms of steep, bracken- and heather-covered headlands, at the end of a lane's tunnel of trees, as the backcloth to the wind-forked skeleton of a pine. Or green in tiny harbours where fishing- and pleasure-boats rock their masts. Or frothing like ginger beer at the feet of tall northern cliffs. Or grey and brown beneath the jetties and cranes of St Helier's dockland. However far one may travel inland it can still be heard breaking and its phosphorescence glows on the dark horizon at night. It can be smelt, stinging in the nostrils or tasted on the lips in winter gales.

No less ubiquitous is the island granite. It is to be found not only along the coast, but inland, breaking out of the ground in sheer, red escarpments. It is the stone from which farmhouse, church and manor were built, as well as those incredible Jersey walls which seem like four-dimensional jigsaw puzzles. And in hedgerows it lurks under a thick overlay of moss, grass and bramble to tear at the paintwork of an incautiously driven car. In great cubic blocks it has been formed into the piers of

9

harbours and, in slabs, into pavements. Outside the houses it is made into rockeries; within, it has been used to construct great, deep fireplaces.

Island life breeds a hardness. The coalition of man, soil and sea is at best an unstable one, existing from necessity not desire and constantly breached by the two stronger at the expense of the weaker partner. The Jerseyman has long learnt to seize the main chance when it offered itself. So he has not only been farmer and fisherman, but also privateer—which is merely a legalised pirate—and smuggler. Many of the island's finest houses were built on the proceeds of salted cod and contraband. Today he is as likely to be a St Helier business-man, a lawyer, a banker, a hotelier or a motor mechanic as farmer or fisherman. Yet the elements remain in his soul and will even summon him back when he has decided to leave his island.

The geographical fact of insularity has allowed the island to develop as supremely itself. Separated from England by 80 miles of some of the most capricious seas in the world, the island's sole tie with it—and that by a chance of history, not annexation or right of conquest—is in the Crown. Even then it is through a subsidiary title, that of Duke of Normandy, not as sovereign of England, Wales, Scotland or Northern Ireland. Often, indeed, Britain has seemed an enemy. France, on the other hand, actually was one and, though so much closer, failed to exert a permanent influence. The language the Jerseyman spoke was certainly not English, but neither was it the French of France.

His political independence arose logically from the convergence of these various factors, so that it became long ago a simple axiom of existence, not an idea put into practice. He and his island were different. And that was that. This uniqueness proclaimed itself not only in language but also in institutions, cultural heritage, religious attitudes. The island has its own parliament, raises its own taxes, makes its own laws and administers them through its own justices.

Jersey attracts something like a million tourists a year; it is an international banking centre, and would-be immigrants queue up to be allowed entry both for themselves and their money. St Helier is filled with expensive shops, its narrow streets are clogged with cars; there is a constant clamour for yacht moorings in the harbours, and private aircraft stand in parked ranks at the airport.

In all this lies the basic enigma of the island. In a world of overpoweringly vaster entities, when the odds appear to be stacked against the small and the insular, Jersey is not only surviving but prospering.

Yet a reservation needs to be entered. Obvious trappings of prosperity against a backdrop of such scenic splendour must lead the casual observer to suppose that all is contentment and that the inhabitants of Jersey live an idyllic existence. This is partly, but not entirely, the case. The government is by no means the despotism it is sometimes represented to be; it is, however, ultra-conservative and prone to paternalism. As is often the case with government by amateurs, its members are too much swayed by the opinions of its own experts, themselves fallible. There has been a great complacency towards social problems which for some inflict a hardship close to desperation and have led to many leaving their native home, although it is unlikely they will ever be allowed to return.

Much of the present wealth comes from sources alien to the nature of Jerseymen and its benefits are felt by the few rather than the many. Frequently, the bringers of that wealth are themselves not only alien but openly contemptuous of the islanders. They must appear to the men who have inhabited and nourished the same plot of earth for well over ten centuries as usurpers and invaders. And, like all invaders, there is nothing to stop these latest ones from getting up and going away, wiping out the prosperity overnight and leaving the island to struggle—an underprivileged backwater—for subsistence. This book is not by its nature a sociological dissertation, but it would be wrong if the vista were allowed to appear as entirely unclouded and serene.

1 THE LIE OF THE LAND

JERSEY is the largest and most southerly of the Channel Islands—among them Guernsey, Alderney and Sark—which nestle in the Bay of St Michel off the north-west coast of France. Lying 100 miles south of Portland Bill, Jersey is the southernmost point in the British Isles, but is considerably closer to France, some 15 miles away. The Normandy beaches are visible on a clear day and many of the island's proper names are derived from the little towns along that part of the French coast.

ROCKS AND TIDES

The island, a great oblong of rock measuring roughly 12 by 6 miles, with an area of some 45 square miles, was once part of the continent of Europe. It is composed of igneous rocks—those which have at some stage been molten: syenites, diorites and rhyolites—granitic rocks of red, blue, grey and purple overall appearance. Part of the west is shale and part of the east conglomerate; sandstone and lava are also present—all betraying the action of a volcano in the past.

The rock formations are pre-Cretaceous, that is, 100–200 million years old. The granites in particular have been shown to be part of such rocks found on the Normandy coast. Until about 8,000 years ago, a great afforested plain joined France and Britain, and something of these forests can still be seen. Occasionally wind and sea have combined to scour the beach at St Ouen's Bay, which faces the Atlantic on the Jersey coast,

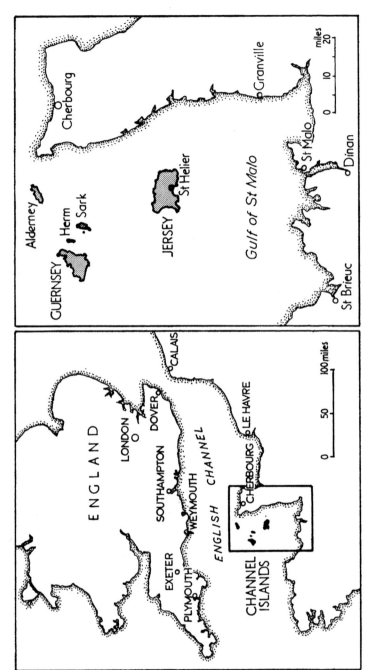

Jersey in relation to the other Channel Islands

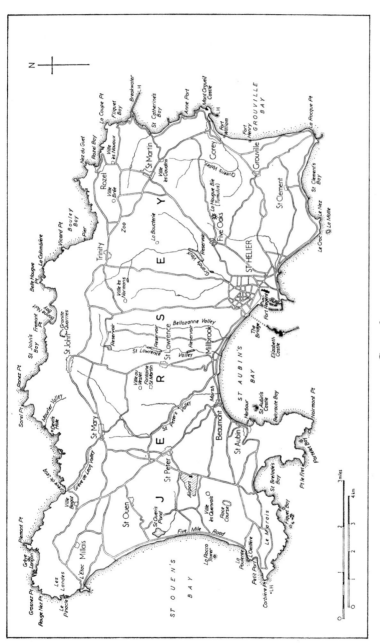

General map

and there beneath sand and shingle, as though left by a ruthless woodsman, stumps of trees protrude from a peaty bed. At that time the Seine, sweeping west, had its estuary on the Atlantic, between what is now Cornwall and Brittany. With the melting of the ice-caps, the waters rose, dividing Guernsey, Alderney and Sark from the mainland, but leaving Jersey temporarily connected.

Habitation of the region goes back at least 100,000 years and the first inhabitants of the land which was to become Jersey were Neanderthal. At La Cotte de St Brelade, a craggy head-land in the west of the island, some 10,000 worked flints have been found, with stone hammers and traces of mammoth, woolly rhinoceros, great elk and deer. Jersey's separation from the continent is thought to have come about in a great storm, as indicated by cooking middens having been suddenly abandoned and utensils filled with blown sand. No such signs of habitation have appeared elsewhere in the Channel Islands, leading to the supposition that they were already separated at that period. Cut off from the mainland, Jersey too became uninhabited.

Over the course of centuries, the waters began to retreat once more. On the cliffs of the island's north coast, bands of pebbles, worn smooth by tidal action, can be found at 130ft, 60ft and 30ft above the present high-tide levels. The Channel Islands are still subject to enormous tides, the highest rising as much as 40ft. This is because the waters flow in two directions: eastward from the Atlantic and westward from the North Sea via the Straits of Dover. The westerly flowing seas are partly constrained by the jutting arm of the Cherbourg peninsula, so that they escape in a great cascade called the Race of Alderney, a fast-moving current capable of driving a large ship before it.

Plate 1 St Helier: (*above*) the harbour with Elizabeth Castle in the background; (*below*) sailing boats in the yacht harbour. On the skyline are some of the buildings of the new entertainment complex at Fort Regent.

Plate 2 St Helier: (*above left*) a corner of Royal Square; (*above right*) the statue of George II, dressed as a Roman senator, faces down Royal Square; (*below*) Broad Street

ISLAND LANDSCAPE

The action of the seas gouged out a sharp and rugged coastline. In the north the cliffs of solid rock rise 250–460ft above sea level and are fissured with caves. Farther east are small rocky coves and inlets, mostly sandy but some, like Bouley Bay, of shingle. The land slopes southward to the sea, each bay demarcated by a rocky headland. At low tides the shoreline appears as rock-strewn as a lunar landscape, and in the east of the island it is said that a raised natural causeway, La Planche— by which it was believed to be possible in earlier times to walk across to France—can still be discerned as a darker line on the water. In the south of the island the sea-bed is, as Balleine says, 'never far from the keel of a boat'. Two of the offshore reefs, the Minquiers and the Ecréhous, which lie some miles from the coast and are large enough to be habitable, come under the Bailiwick of Jersey.

Inland the Jersey landscape appears much as it has done for centuries: open fields divided by banked hedges, with scattered farmsteads and collections of houses grouped at crossroads surrounding the parish church and *salle paroissiale*.

CLIMATE

Canted towards the sun, sheltered by the encircling arm of the French coast and warmed by the Gulf Stream, Jersey has a specially favourable climate, with mild winters and long-lasting summers. The prevailing winds are south-westerly, giving an average rainfall of 34in.

The annual average of 1,915·11 hours of sunshine puts the island among the top three sunniest places in the British Isles, but the midsummer climate can be unreliable. Even on a brilliant summer's day, the high, seaborne winds may keep down the temperatures on the beaches. The mean annual temperature is, however, several degrees higher than in Britain and, with the warm weather starting earlier, the local conditions are exploited by farmers and growers in getting their produce—principally potatoes, tomatoes and flowers—to British markets in advance of home crops.

PLANT AND ANIMAL LIFE

From early spring, heather and fern cover the hillsides, and wild daffodils fill the deeper meadows in February. Palm trees and eucalyptus thrive in the mild climate, while hydrangeas grow in profusion and camellias often bloom at Christmastime.

There is a variety of fauna common to Britain, though the hare has died out; as well as bank voles and green lizards which are found in France—further evidence that Jersey was not always an island. The Jersey shrew and a local toad called the *crapaud*, which has become the nickname of a Jerseyman, are species unique to the island; so too was the red-legged partridge, now extinct.

Fish abound in the warm, clear water. Shellfish are particularly plentiful; apart from lobster, crayfish, prawns and limpets, these include the ormer (*Haliotis tuberculata*) or *oreille-de-mer* and the spider—or 'soldier'—crab, both of which are very popular local delicacies.

2 CROSSCURRENTS OF HISTORY

EARLY SETTLERS

JERSEY'S location on so many sea routes led to a succession
of wanderers visiting the island, among them a dark race,
miscalled 'Iberians' but originating in the Middle East,
who moved from the Mediterranean up the Atlantic seaboard
about 2000 BC. These people possessed more than the rudi-
ments of civilisation and Jersey abounds in the megaliths and
dolmens which marked their passage. They made simple pottery, cut and polished stone—their flintwork is of high quality
and the material must have been imported, as there is none on
the island; they hunted, grew corn, grinding it in stone querns,
built huts and gathered shellfish.

They were followed by the Gauls, who brought Druidism to
Jersey, and in due course by the Romans. Roman potsherds,
bronze rings, an iron blade and a coin of the Emperor Com-
modus AD 185 were found in the north-west corner of St
Ouen's Bay on the west coast, where the 200ft Pinnacle Rock
was probably used as a signal station. In the Antonine Itinerary,
a Roman guide book and work of navigational instructions, a
group of islands lying between the Isle of Wight and Ushant
are named Riduna, Sarnia and Caesarea, and assumed to be
respectively Alderney, Guernsey and Jersey. Although Caesar
never visited the island, the name persists today in local societies
such as the Caesarean Cycling Club, Caesarean Angling Club
and Caesarean Tennis Club.

In the sixth century AD, the island was known as Angia or Agna. The name 'Jersey', often spelt with a 'G', did not appear until about 1025. 'Gers' may come from the old Frisian for grass, and '-ey' is a Norse suffix denoting an island, so that 'Gers-ey' meant 'grassy isle'. It has also been suggested that it might have been called 'Geirr's Island', Geirr being a Norwegian personal name.

With the eclipse of the Roman Empire, Clovis's Salian Franks spread westward from the Rhine and established their dominion over Jersey. They were thought to have been responsible for the island's division into twelve parts, each with its own assembly of elders, which is evident in the present-day island parishes. The Franks were mainly preoccupied with family squabbles among their leaders, during the course of which Armorica, now Brittany, became depopulated and devastated by the fighting armies. When news of this deserted region reached the Britons, at that time hard pressed by the Saxons, a migration began. It was their passage southward which led to men like St Sampson, St Marcouf, St Helier and St Magloire visiting the Channel Islands and converting them to Christianity. The old harsh paganism died hard. It was said that St Sampson had to bribe Jersey children with the promise of a medal to keep them away from the pagan sun festival which corresponded with the Christian Christmas.

The first effort to wean the people of the island from the Celtic church and drag them within the ambit of Catholicism was made by Charlemagne in the eighth century when he sent the Abbot of Fontenelle to bring Jersey under the See of Coutances, a little town on the nearby Normandy coast.

In the meantime Norsemen from Scandinavia had taken possession of that part of the Frankish kingdom then called Neustria, now Normandy, where they established themselves in such strength that the king of the Franks made terms with them. He offered his daughter in marriage to the Viking chieftain, giving him the title of Duke of Normandy. By 933 the islands had been annexed to their duchy and in 1030 Duke Robert I—Robert le Diable—paid them an unintended visit. On his way to England to support Edgar Atheling against Canute, he was driven off by a storm on the Sussex coast and reached the haven of 'Gersui'.

THE NORMANS

Although the Normans were to leave a permanent mark on the islands, initially they made little impact and even today the feeling in Jersey remains more akin to that of Britanny than Normandy—closer, that is to say, to the Celtic influence than to the French.

Following Duke William's northern adventure in 1066, the Channel Islands were not attached to his new English kingdom but remained part of the Norman duchy. The islanders paid their taxes to Rouen, whose mint produced the local currency, but Jersey already had a basic system of government and perhaps for this reason feudalism was never fully imposed upon its people. The ancient ceremony of *l'ouie de paroisse*—'in the hearing of the parish'—was allowed to continue. Under it all legal acts of importance had to take place in the parish church, officially before the whole community— an early instance of democracy in practice.

Serfdom, as such, was never introduced into the island, though seigneurial tenants were required to cut their lord's hay, to cart his wood and wine, and to clean out his *colombier* or pigeon-loft, a practice retained up to the eighteenth century.

At the same time the islanders claimed and were granted a number of inalienable rights. They were not required to do military service, although they undertook to accompany their

23

duke to England 'if need be'. They could not be tried by any court outside the island or by any law but their own, though the seigneurs possessed and exercised gibbet-rights.

There were in the island a few fiefs appertaining to the duke himself, so-called royal fiefs, but for the most part estates were so small that their seigneurs were not required to render knight-service and paid a tax in lieu. They had, however, a number of quaint obligations, such as that of the Seigneur of Rozel, who had to ride into the sea up to the girth of his horse to meet the duke, should he visit the island.

For the ordinary people, even the tenants of a royal fief, life must have continued much as before. They cultivated their land with ox-drawn ploughs, paid their taxes and rendered such services as were demanded by their seigneurs.

The abbots and bishops had also been given fiefs and manor houses and, unlike the Celtic priests and monks who had been close to the ordinary people, they acted the *grand seigneur* and demanded taxes and services from their tenants as the barons did. Hatred of this situation turned some of the islanders back to an earlier religion altogether: in the witches' covens the new was repudiated and the old invoked. Satan, the great enemy of Christianity, was seen as an ally and became 'the Lord of Earth'—the people's earth which their overlords were stealing from them.

While gradually reshaping the legal, social and economic life of the island, the Normans would have had little effect ethnically upon the islanders. There were simply too few of them and the seigneurs would hardly have sought consorts among their tenantry; even natural children or products of *droit de seigneur* would have scarcely altered the island blood.

The principal manifestation of their presence was in their rebuilding of the churches: by tearing down the wooden chantry chapels of Jersey and reconstructing them in the granite which stands today, the Normans—as was perhaps their intention—impressed upon the people's minds the permanence of the new order.

ENGLISH SUZERAINTY

In 1203 King John was losing his French possessions and there was a threatening pro-French party among the Jersey seigneurs. To bring them to heel he sent a punitive expedition to the island the following year, under the renegade Benedictine, Eustace the Monk. A defence was attempted by the Seigneur of St Ouen—one of the early de Carterets, the family whose name was to become so renowned and at times so reviled in the island's history; but after the incursion it was said that 'nothing was left to burn'.

By 1207 the islands were firmly under English control and suzerainty. De Suligny, despatched by the king to become Warden of the Isles, brought with him a strong force whose purpose was both to subdue the island internally and to defend it from external enemies. Jersey's role was to be a dual one: on the one hand it was an outpost, uncomfortably close to the French coast; on the other it was to strive to assert and maintain its identity, sometimes coming into conflict with the very power on whom it was dependent for its protection.

Rights and privileges

King John realised, as Duke William had done, the folly of alienating the islanders who were within such easy reach of enemy shores. He therefore granted them concessions he would not otherwise have done: he left the basically Norman law unaltered; he confirmed their customs and privileges; he even allowed them to remain under the diocese of Coutances, as well as restoring the rights and possessions of the Norman abbeys in the islands.

While the sense of nationhood grew—as early as 1323 the term 'the community of the islands' was used in legal documents—the struggle for independence continued. Edward I sought to abrogate the islands' rights by having them proved at law, but a commission of lawyers sent for this purpose encountered a set and unswerving resistance among the people. Otto de Grandison, whom Edward appointed as Warden of the Isles, conducted a campaign of high-handed terror which led to open revolt and to his recall. The next warden, before being accepted, had to swear to guard and maintain the islands' privileges, liberties and ancient customs, but the islanders' discontent persisted through the ensuing reigns.

In July 1341, Edward III conceded what the islands had long demanded: 'Considering how faithfully the beloved men of our Isles have ever maintained their loyalty towards the Kings of England, and how much they have suffered in defence of their islands and our rights and honour, we concede for ourselves and for our heirs that they hold and retain all privileges, immunities and customs granted by our Forebears.'

Though the last Plantagenet kings and their Lancastrian successors confirmed what had been granted, the islands were far enough away from England for the wardens to behave as a law unto themselves. Against these petty despots the islands had to embark on protracted litigations and appeals to the Privy Council in London.

External threats

In 1337, following an attempt by David Bruce, the deposed Scots king, to take the island, Edward III ordered all Jerseymen capable of bearing arms to be levied. At this period too the great defensive structures were being built: Grosnez in the north-west of the island; Châtel Sedement in the north-east, and the castle of Gorey in the east.

Du Guesclin, among the most famous of French soldiers, left the siege of Brest in 1373 and, accompanied by the Duc de Bourbon, sailed for Jersey with 2,000 gendarmes and 600 bowmen. He attacked the great fortress of Gorey and, when the assault failed, his sappers began digging deep tunnels beneath it. In the end the defenders, though in no real danger, negotiated for peace; they handed over hostages and agreed to pay a ransom by instalments. The whole discreditable affair led to the warden being dismissed and the Bailiff of Jersey, who was head of the civil administration, was sent to the Tower of Londou.

Pero Niño, the Spanish soldier of fortune, with Hector de Pontbriant, raided the island in 1406, defeating the Jersey militia after a bloody fight. He extorted a ransom of 10,000 golden crowns as well as an annual tribute of twelve lances, twelve axes, twelve bows and twelve trumpets.

In 1461, the castle of Gorey was surprised and taken by a French force under Jean de Carbonnel. Although the militia held out in one small enclave in the west, the island quickly fell and remained in French possession for seven years. The St Ouen detachment of militiamen who participated in Jersey's eventual liberation earned for themselves the privilege of parading on the right of the line thereafter.

A respite from front-line dangers began in 1483 when Pope Sixtus IV set his seal on a Bull of Neutrality for the islands, by which they would be excluded from any future wars between France and England.

Command and defence

The Warden of the Isles, specifically a soldier, was appointed in England, while the bailiff, in charge of civil affairs, was a local man. By the reign of Henry VII Jersey and Guernsey each had a separate governor, in place of the overall warden, and the bailiff was often seen as a threat to his power. A Jersey governor, Baker, produced a false letter purporting to show that the bailiff was offering to betray Gorey Castle to the French; only the efforts of his wife, Margaret de Carteret, saved him. She hastened to London and persuaded the Privy

27

Council to forbid his trial and to remove Baker from office. One bailiff was kept waiting for twelve years by Cardinal Wolsey when he went to plead for the removal of another despotic governor, Vaughan; he had to shout his challenge across the Court of Star Chamber before he got a hearing from Henry VIII's chancellor.

The governor of Jersey from 1537 to 1550 was Edward Seymour, brother of Jane Seymour. By the 1530s confidence in the state of neutrality was on the wane and a commission was sent from England to look at the island's defences. Grosnez and Sedement had fallen into decay, but Gorey—the castle known as Mont Orgueil since the French occupation—afforded vital observation of the seas as far as the coast of France. To this fortress Seymour added the tower named after him and he also fortified a reef of rock off St Aubins, some miles to the west. Although he was accused of being extortionate in his demands on the islanders for money and resources to build up these defences, his endeavours were justified in 1549 when the militia, remodelled into twelve parish bands, drove off another French invasion attempt, inflicting heavy losses.

Mont Orgueil was subsequently saved from destruction when Sir Walter Ralegh, as governor, wrote to Queen Elizabeth praising it as a 'stately fort' and adding 'it were a pity to cast it down'. During her reign, another castle, named after her, was constructed off the St Helier foreshore.

THE REFORMATION

The religious vicissitudes of the rest of Europe were reflected in the islands. Henry VIII, according to Balleine, bribed the Pope, Roderigo Borgia, into a Bull transferring them to the administration of Winchester, though for fifty years longer the Bishop of Coutances continued to confirm, ordain and collect fees. The fact of this change, however, was used as an excuse for keeping the islands under English religious sway when the king broke with Rome.

There were no strong objections among the islanders when measures to protestantise them were taken by the Council of Regency under Edward VI, and the Act of Uniformity and Cranmer's prayer book, translated into French, were adopted with only a very few rectors refusing to conform.

The wave of Protestantism which broke over the island was not in fact, as Balleine says, 'the easy Anglicanism of England'; it came from French sources, Calvinist and Huguenot. Jacques Le Fèvre's New Testament in French reached the island and trained Frenchmen arrived to 'expound the Word of God to the people according to the Gospels'. Very soon Jersey's most important families, such as the Lemprières and the de Carterets, were avowed Protestants.

Attempts by Mary I to bring about a reversion to Catholicism failed. A Catholic dean was appointed, but the governor, Hugh Paulet, was shrewd enough to give the post to his own brother, over whom he could exercise control. Most islanders felt under no constraint to give up their reformed faith.

The accession of Elizabeth allowed them full freedom. The Acts of Supremacy and Uniformity were enforced, but the practice of the island was notably Huguenot and Calvinist in tenor. In 1562, a Huguenot minister, Guillaume Morise, became the rector of St Helier and the Calvinist system of church government was introduced.

In 1617 James I sent a royal commission to Jersey to see how Anglicanism could be grafted on to the Huguenot church. A dean, Bandinel, was specially selected to enforce Anglicanism in the island, but his method of doing so quickly antagonised the people and, apart from abolishing Calvinist government and introducing the prayer book, had no lasting effects.

In the period immediately preceding the Civil War, the island's religious forces concentrated on the eradication from their midst of witchcraft and satanism—never far below the surface. The witches were hunted down and found in the most august quarters. One, Marie Renouf, was the granddaughter of the rector of St John's; another the wife of a prominent landowner. Though torture was never permitted in Jersey and the sentence on conviction was death, many made full and boastful confessions of their dealings with Satan and the dark powers.

THE CIVIL WAR

Sir Philippe de Carteret, as Bailiff of Jersey, wished to keep the island neutral during the Civil War while at the same time remaining loyal to the king. However, his nephew, Sir George de Carteret, who was a Royalist naval officer, was engaged in running munitions from France, via Jersey, to the West Country. Sir Philippe refused to intervene to end this trade, and was brought before the Jersey parliament, the States, to explain his conduct. He answered with perfect constitutional correctness that 'the island has nothing to do with parliament but only with the King in Council'. What followed was as much a product of the resentment built up against the de Carterets, who had come to regard themselves virtually as hereditary rulers, as with wider political causes. Two of the bailiff's rivals in the States, Michel Lemprière and Henri Dumaresq, called out units of the militia and Sir Philippe was forced to take refuge in Elizabeth Castle, while his wife took over Mont Orgueil. By turning the castle guns on Parliamentarist ships pursuing a Royalist frigate, Sir Philippe finally abandoned his position of neutrality.

Parliament had meanwhile sent the Earl of Warwick to Jersey to become the new governor. De Carteret attempted a sortie to retake St Helier, but the citizens and militia turned out in force to repel him. He died later in an epidemic which afflicted his garrison.

An officer had been commissioned by Parliament to retake the two castles, but there was now a declining enthusiasm for the struggle between parliamentary and royalist aims, and the task was regarded as hopeless, since the garrisons were being supplied by sea. The attacking forces began to melt away. In these circumstances, the Royalists saw their opportunity and, in November 1645, a scratch force of English, Irish, Scots and French were sent from St Malo under the command of Sir George de Carteret. The island fell after little resistance, though there was a poor response when he tried to raise a Royalist force there. The people were sick of the war and thereafter de Carteret turned to privateering—or what was in fact unabashed piracy—as a way of supporting himself and, to a degree, the Royalist funds. At the same time his attempt to bring to trial those who had backed the Parliamentary cause was thwarted in London by threats to kill three Royalist prisoners for every man executed by Sir George.

In April 1646 Charles, the young Prince of Wales, fleeing from the West of England after the catastrophe of the Battle of Worcester, roused the flagging interest of the islanders and quickly won over the leadership of town and country to the Royalist cause. This was somewhat modified after his departure when there was talk of a plan to sell the islands to France to raise funds.

In the meantime, Lemprière and Dumaresq were in London trying to stir Parliament into taking action to recover the island and install them in power. Various projects were put in hand but had to be shelved on the outbreak of the Second Civil War.

When news of the execution of Charles I reached Jersey, de Carteret at once had the young prince proclaimed king, so that the island became the first part of the royal dominions to do so. In September 1649, Charles paid a second short visit to Jersey and then departed for Scotland to meet the Scottish Commissioners who looked likely to give real assistance to his cause.

It was another two years before the Cromwellian forces were ready to settle with this unruly island and then it was de Carteret's privateering which directly stimulated action. He had reinforced his local forces with Scandinavian mercenaries, whose thieving made them extremely unpopular with the islanders. They proved no match for the 2,600 men of the New Model Army, under Heane and the redoubtable Admiral Blake, who were sent to reduce the island. Within twenty-four hours all but the two castles were in Parliamentarist hands. Mont Orgueil capitulated quickly thereafter, but Heane had to send home for heavy siege guns to subdue Elizabeth Castle.

Sir George de Carteret, in charge of the defenders, negotiated with such success that he retained all his own property and shortly afterwards left for France where he became an admiral in the French Navy. He had already received from the king, as a reward for his loyalty, lands in America which he called New Jersey.

Under the rule of Parliament, relations between the islanders and the troops were not bad, though there was a certain amount of religious friction since the Roundheads regarded the island's Calvinism as little better than sacrilegiously ostentatious. To prevent incidents, Heane himself had to attend the island churches—which must have provided him with periods of aching boredom since he understood no word of the French in which the services were conducted.

The Restoration was generally welcomed, even though it meant the return of the unpopular and arrogant de Carteret whose influence now became supreme. The king presented Jersey with a silver-gilt mace, bearing the words: 'Not all doth he deem worthy of such honour', which leads to the view that he was not unaware of the paltriness of the gift; it was, however, borne before the bailiff on all important occasions thereafter.

Threats from external sources remained. In 1688 there were anxious times when William of Orange landed at Torbay and an attempt to seize Jersey in the name of the departing Stuart monarch, James II, was frustrated. The ringleaders were captured and Catholic regiments in the island disarmed. A period of peace and stability then commenced which was to last nearly a century.

WAR BETWEEN BRITAIN AND FRANCE

With the outbreak of war, the island's profitable privateering recommenced, causing such chagrin to the French that in 1779 they sent a reprisal force, under the Prince of Nassau, to invade Jersey. This attack was repulsed by the militia and led to another spate of defensive building, with a string of Martello watch towers along the south coast. A French officer wrote at this time: 'The habit of facing the dangers of the sea has made the inhabitants of Jersey very brave. They form a body of militia which is well disciplined and good in marksmanship and which has been capable, almost alone, of repulsing any enemy which has descended upon it.'

In a second invasion attempt, in 1781, the French at least succeeded in gaining a foothold on the island when, in the early hours of 6 January, some 1,000 men under Baron de Rullecourt landed in the east. By sunrise they had reached St Helier unchecked. Here de Rullecourt presented himself at the home of Moses Corbet, who as lieutenant-governor was commander of the defence forces. The unhappy Corbet was dragged from bed and, with bare white legs beneath nightshirt and hair tumbled under sleeping-cap, faced the crisply uniformed Frenchman. Thus disadvantaged, he accepted de Rullecourt's assertion that the French forces were present in overwhelming numbers and signed the island away to him.

The bluff might have succeeded totally but for twenty-four-year-old Major Francis Peirson who, deciding that the capitulation order was invalid as having been obtained under duress, mustered local forces for a stand. The French soldiers were corralled into the Royal Square in St Helier to be mown down by the British infantry, while militia artillery poured down shot from the heights above. By the end of the so-called Battle of Jersey both de Rullecourt and Peirson had been killed, but the French were defeated. Corbet was duly summoned before a court of inquiry in London and relieved of his governorship, though not otherwise punished.

During the years that followed, the island's role of outpost became offensive rather than defensive. In Jersey as throughout Europe there had been a growth of political consciousness and the first local reaction to the French Revolution of 1789 was to welcome it as the realisation of 'the Rights of Man'. Revolutionary excesses soon alienated this feeling and Jersey became a refuge for émigré aristocrats. About 3,500 of these men who were of military age enlisted in a contingent to support the monarchist resistance. In July 1795, with a similar force from Guernsey, they landed in Quiberon Bay in Brittany, where the Republican troops made short and bloody work of them.

Through the Napoleonic Wars, privateering by the islanders again provided an irritant to the French and there was such lively expectation of invasion that a particularly active and able soldier, General Conway, was sent to Jersey to speedily organise its defences. Among the measures he took was the fortifying of the rocky outcrop overlooking St Helier on the seaward side. Work began in 1806, the labour being supplied by the islanders, and Fort Regent, as it was called, was completed in 1814 at a cost of £375,203. The dynamic Conway also organised a telegraph system by which the lookout on Mont Orgueil could signal the movement of any ships out of St Malo. Transmission via Grosnez and Sark to St Peter Port in Guernsey, where a British squadron lay in wait, was said to take only a quarter of an hour.

The anticipated assault never came, though the island's

Plate 3 Elizabeth Castle, St Helier: (*left*) viewed from the harbour

te 3 (*right*) The Hermitage. was here that the legendary Helier was said to have en murdered by pirates in sixth century

Plate 4 Two local sports: (*above*) sand-racing at St Ouen's Bay. Meetings for cars – specially modified for the conditions – and motorcycles take place regularly through the summer organised by the Jersey Motor Cycle and Light Car Club; (*below*) The waiters' race. This is a popular annual event organised by the Jersey Hotel and Guest Houses Association.

smuggling and privateering activities, which were affecting Napoleon's attempts to prevent continental commerce with Britain, led him to observe bitterly: 'France can no longer tolerate this nest of brigands and assassins, Europe must be purged. Jersey is England's shame.'

The victory of Waterloo, the Second Treaty of Paris and the gradual diminution of hostility between France and Britain marked the end of Jersey's existence as a front-line outpost.

INTERNAL AFFAIRS

The 1820s saw the islanders once more challenging the Houses of Parliament; an Act had been passed prohibiting foreign corn from being brought into the Channel Islands at times when there was a ban on importing it in Britain. The Jerseymen resented the notion that the British parliament could pass measures affecting their own island, and the stubbornness of their opposition was such that the law was changed.

During the first half of the nineteenth century, retired British army officers had begun to take up residence in Jersey, seeing it as a desirable retreat where their fixed incomes were likely to be worth slightly more than in England. These men took every opportunity to remind any listening Jerseyman how much more efficiently public affairs were managed in Britain.

One islander who was converted to these views was Abraham Le Cras and his noisy declaration that self-government in Jersey was a sham led to a royal commission being set up to investigate the island's affairs. There were certainly abuses resulting from the party factionalism which had split the people to the point where even local judges were party men. The commission recommended that there should in future be three Crown-appointed judges for Jersey; a properly organised professional police force, and a police court. The Privy Council issued orders to bring these arrangements into being, but they were never carried out. Some 7,000 local people, resenting British interference, signed a petition asking for the orders to be set aside. Finally, a compromise was reached when the States passed a law setting up the police force, though only for St Helier, as well as a police court.

Le Cras, not to be deterred from his campaign, brought a Bill before the States to amend the constitution and allow the introduction of the Crown-selected judges. A plebiscite on the issue was held and, when this resulted in an overwhelming vote in favour of retaining the island judges, Le Cras gave up the struggle.

There were further instances of ill-feeling between the islanders and the British. In 1843, Major-General Sir William Napier, a hero of the Peninsular War who was appointed lieutenant-governor of Guernsey, began treating the local authorities and the courts with such disdain that the Home Office in London feared an open rebellion and imprudently sent a force of 600 men to keep control. This step further injured the Channel Islanders by its imputation on their loyalty, and the local situation was fast deteriorating.

Eventually, in 1846, Sir George Grey, Home Secretary in the new Liberal Government, wisely suggested that Queen Victoria herself should visit the islands. She arrived in Guernsey, un-announced, in the royal yacht, and received a tumultuous welcome from the garrison and people. She then passed on to Jersey, the first monarch to visit the island since Charles II. The newly built south pier at St Helier harbour, where she landed, was renamed Victoria Pier. After meeting civic dignitaries, she drove to Mont Orgueil and re-embarked on her yacht. The whole visit lasted hardly more than four hours and covered only a small area of the island—though remote hamlets far off the royal route hurriedly built triumphal arches—but it had the effect of affirming the islanders' loyalty to the Crown.

3 AN ISLAND PEOPLE

JERSEY emerged into the twentieth century with a distinct 'national' personality and with the self-confidence which comes from an unshakable sense of identity. The island had its own institutions and language, and had developed a way of life which, in its social customs, religious attitudes and architectural style, reflected the people's individuality and self-reliance. The Jerseyman's pride in his island was such that he could bear no criticism and, until a few years ago, people who ventured to express the least displeasure were told: 'Well, there's a boat in the morning . . .'

Lemprière, himself a Jerseyman, sums up his compatriots as short of stature, 'dark and not especially good-looking', and they are, he declares, acquisitive, thrifty to the point of meanness, but also enterprising and informed by a spirit of hardy independence. Each separate characteristic has its source in the Jerseyman's history, the sheer daily realities of island life and the racial mix from which he sprang; to this last there had been added fresh transfusions of Norman, Breton, English and Irish blood. His passionate attachment to land, property and family may have come in part from his Norman inheritance, but also from an awareness that in the very worst of times it is these that support him and provide subsistence.

On the lighter side, the Jerseyman has enormous personal charm, loves laughter and is, as Lemprière says, 'hospitable and makes a good host'. He is too one of nature's democrats and, if he boasts infuriatingly of an ancient lineage, it is largely

39

because others have placed importance on such things. In Britain barely half a dozen families can claim an ancestry going back to the Conquest; in Jersey there are scores who can show a pedigree of far greater antiquity. Local names like Ozouf or Renouf, for example, are corruptions of the Viking Oswulf and Renwulf.

TRADITIONAL LIFE

From the earliest days, the land and the sea were exploited to the utmost for the islanders' subsistence, and from them came the traditional customs: the ormering parties, held when the *oreille-de-mer* were gathered; the Grands Charrues, celebrations after ploughing; 'black butter' nights when a conserve was made from apples and cider, and the days spent 'vraicking'— collecting seaweed from the beaches to use as fertiliser on the soil.

One great occasion of Jersey life was the annual parade, inspection and trooping the colour in honour of the sovereign's official birthday, when everyone repaired to St Helier for the day, even work on the farms being abandoned, to watch not only the battalions of the regular army stationed on the island but particularly the Royal Militia—a proud reminder of the astonishing fact that this small island had almost invariably deterred whatever forces were sent against it.

There was some traditional folk music, though hardly any has survived, and legends, playlets and monologues in the Jersey-French patois.

RELIGION

In religious matters, Jersey presents a society which has constantly reverted to a more rigid creed. Successive generations had witnessed the establishment in the island's church of practices corresponding more and more closely with the Episcopalian Anglicanism of England, but in the latter part of the eighteenth century Wesleyan Methodism spread to the Channel Islands. Brackenbury, the ardent young squire of Raithby sent by Wesley as his apostle, began holding services at 3 Royal Square, St Helier; among his earliest converts was a young Jerseyman, Jean de Quetteville, who was able, unlike Brackenbury, to preach in the vernacular.

In 1787 John Wesley himself, aged eighty-four, visited the island; besides preaching to large congregations on each of the seven days of his stay, he was entertained at the homes of many influential islanders. The faith which he and his followers promulgated became something of a local 'established church' and Methodist chapels and tabernacles appeared all over Jersey, often outstripping the parish churches in size and attendance. Grove Place Methodist Church in St Helier is the island's largest place of worship.

Methodism has frequently been blamed for the unswerving puritanism and strict Sabbath observance which impeded attempts to liberalise local attitudes towards licensing hours, gambling and betting. Many of the island's leaders are Methodists and until recent years a markedly anti-Catholic bias was prevalent, even extending into legislation.

In these religious attitudes, and in their sinister obverse of superstition and witchcraft—which are very much alive—one is encountering something very fundamental in the Jerseyman's character.

ARCHITECTURE

This same characteristic manifests itself in some of the island's architecture, particularly in those farmsteads which, when the planked gates are closed over the entrance arches, present such a forbidding aspect, like that of a small fortress.

By the eighteenth century, the farming population had become the leaders of the parish assemblies, the churches and the courts, and they constructed houses befitting their new status. In these, walls of granite 3ft thick were usually pierced along the front by nine windows, four on the ground floor, five on the upper. An ample kitchen with its big open fireplace became the main living room and often had its own bread-oven. A feature of these dwellings, and one unique to the island, were the *benitiers*, or stone niches, which may well have come originally from the churches when the apparatus of the old faith began to be dismantled with the coming of Protestant-ism. There was, besides the invariable large dresser, and, hanging from the ceiling, a rack for bread and the bacon, often home-cured.

The main article of furniture was a massive table of heavy wood at which the family sat and ate, and often remained thereafter—the parlour being kept for such important occasions as weddings, funerals and perhaps Christmas celebrations, so that it always smelt a little musty.

Outbuildings, usually attached to the farmhouse, sometimes forming an L or the three sides of a square, included stabling, storage and cow-barns. Latterly, a room for the *pressoir*, in which cider was made, was added to it.

The building in which all were housed was often completed by a granite archway with a double opening—a larger one for farm vehicles and the smaller for pedestrians; there would usually be a lintel bearing the engraved date of the house's construction and intertwined hearts celebrating the marriage of its first owners.

The roof was sometimes of pantiles, more often of thatch. Where this has been replaced in more recent times by slate, or even sadly by corrugated-iron sheeting, the absence of the thick thatching has left exposed small ledges round the chimneys whose purpose was to give fixings for the thatch, but which have come to be called 'witches perches'.

The eighteenth century also saw the conversion of many of the old Norman manor houses into pseudo châteaux, and the building of fine houses, with granite façades and rectangular shuttered windows, by those who had prospered as sea traders, privateers and smugglers. St Helier has markedly the air of the period, despite crass attempts at modernisation, and has scarcely changed from the town shown in contemporary prints.

LANGUAGE

It was inevitable that France, the nearer neighbour, should have a greater influence on the local tongue. The islands' absorption into the Duchy of Normandy introduced them to the somewhat corrupt French which the Normans had themselves adopted a century earlier. It was this which formed the basis of the Jersey patois, though it is now so different from French in orthography and pronunciation as to be largely incomprehensible to a French-speaking visitor.

In the higher levels of island life—in the courts and in government circles—this rustic tongue was deemed too crude for official use, and high French was employed, as it still is, for many formalities. Newspapers, when they began to appear, were printed in French, though its use in everyday conversation was regarded not merely as a snobbish affectation but as a demonstrable lack of patriotism. Not even Guernsey-French bore more than a basic similarity to the patois, and variations developed between one parish and another, sometimes even in neighbouring ones.

French and its bastard sister, the island patois, continued to be the lingua franca through the centuries and the majority of the people did not understand English. But, as commerce increased, more and more islanders found it necessary to learn it, and men like Sir Philippe and Sir George de Carteret were bilingual.

Today the Jerseyman favours English, which he speaks with an accent comparable to that of Afrikaaner English, though with less broad vowels. He tends to end a sentence in a rising cadence, where an Englishman uses a falling one. When he makes use of unfamiliar polysyllabic words, he will frequently place the accent where it would be in French.

He is given to phrases which are direct interpretations: the word 'me' is put at the beginning of a sentence which expresses an opinion or affirms a taste, corresponding to the French 'moi'; the use of 'eh' at the end of sentences, even when they are non-interrogative, is like the rural Frenchman's 'hein', and the addition of 'but' to an affirmative lends emphasis, as 'But yes!', and is paralleled by the Frenchman's 'mais' used for the same purpose.

Though the island tongue can be said to be a dying language, it may still be heard when people encounter one another in a St Helier street or among groups gathered round the farmhouse fire.

LIFE ON THE LAND

Under Norman law, land had to be shared among all the family at the owner's death. The object of this was to prevent the impoverishment of youngest sons, while at the same time encouraging the growth of a middle class of property owners. It led, however, to the gradual diminution of the size of holdings and the development of that type of strip cultivation still in evidence in parts of the island, particularly in the north-west. As fields grew smaller to the point where they ceased to offer an economic return, there was a tendency to join them together again, so that in deeds describing land the phrase *maintenant reunis en une pièce* recurs.

The comparative mildness of the climate made it possible to double crop, and grass grew all year round to provide feedstuff for cattle. A second advantage rose from the fact of Jersey being an island. Seaweed, which flourishes in the mild waters, provides a cheap form of fertiliser, known locally as *vraic*—and pronounced, approximately, 'wrack'. It is thrown up on the beaches in the winter storms to be gathered by farmers and stacked for the rains to wash out much of the salt. These piles, drying and partly decomposing, giving off a characteristic iodine-like smell, are a familiar sight in the island countryside, especially near the coast.

To begin with, the principal produce was wheat, but by the reign of Edward I the larger estates had already broken down into smaller entities through *partage*, and, with the added handicap of a wheat tax, farmers were forced to look for crops yielding a higher reward proportionate to land area. They therefore began to diversify by growing parsnips—as much a delicacy then as asparagus is today and commanding prices accordingly. For centuries island farming continued on much the same pattern.

Wool

By the fifteenth century agriculture was moving into a new phase destined to make Jersey a household word. The island bred its own strain of sheep, a four-horned curiosity remarked upon by visitors, and from its fleece a local industry began to develop: knitwear, in particular stockings, highly valued in the English markets. The industry rapidly grew to such proportions that petitions were addressed to England to allow wool to be imported to the island to meet the demand.

Soon everyone was busy knitting—men, women and even children. Ten thousand pairs of stockings a week were leaving the island. The knitters did not merely break the Sabbath, they actually took their needles to church with them, where their clicking was said to drown the preacher's voice. Work on the land was threatened and the authorities had to prohibit knitting during the vraicking and harvest seasons. A system of inspection was inaugurated and all stockings of inferior quality confiscated.

The Civil War caused an interruption, but the industry restarted in the 1660s and continued profitable, despite competition from the French, import quotas imposed by Louis XIV's government and a reduction in wool supplies from Britain. A sales policy was adopted and the island products received such enticing names as Rejoicing Widow, Dying Monkey, Amorous Desire, Sad Friend and Mortal Sin; the price was as high as £6.50 a pair. By 1686, Jersey was receiving double the allocation of wool permissible in Charles II's reign and the industry continued to expand.

Cider

Cider-making began to develop from a home product into a local industry in the 1760s. By 1832 half the island land was given over to cider apples and in 1839 some 269,189 gallons of Jersey cider was exported to England. In summer and early autumn the fields were redolent with the sweet, clean smell of cider apples. The pressoirs were originally made of granite and included a double trough and an enormous granite wheel, pulled round by a horse, to crush the apples in the outer trough. This picturesque method of cider-making began to disappear when wooden presses of French or British design were introduced.

Although the manufacture of cider for personal consumption was to continue for some time, proprietary beers, including local brews, were by the turn of the century beginning to replace the Jerseyman's traditional drink, while the growing of cider apples in the larger orchards in the West of England, often from Jersey trees, reduced the export trade.

Potatoes

In 1880, at a Grand Charrue party, a local farmer named de la Haye handed his guests two huge potatoes for their inspection. One of these had no fewer than sixteen eyes. At

46

the table both potatoes were cut up, with an eye in each piece, and the following day they were planted. In the spring of 1881 a huge early crop appeared. The potato was named by de la Haye the Jersey Royal Fluke, later shortened and dignified to the Jersey Royal. Stocks were built up and seedlings sold to other farmers; so began the Jersey new potato trade.

Farmers in the island had been looking for an alternative to the cereals which, since the repeal of the Corn Laws in Britain in the 1840s, had lost their value. They now seemed to have found what they needed and within ten years potato exports had risen to 70,000 tons a year and were bringing in £500,000 to the growers. By 1919 they had attained the £1 million mark and were yearly increasing in value.

Cattle

Until the nineteenth century, a cow was simply part of farm existence, providing milk for the household and perhaps a little for sale. The typical animal was ungainly, high-boned and ragged in form; it was a mixture of many breeds which at one time or another had been brought into the island, and was described by Colonel Le Couteur as the 'Meg Merrilies of the bovine race'.

When a ban on French imports was imposed, Jersey farmers had to improve their own strains and Le Couteur encouraged them to embark on a campaign of scientific breeding. The result was a cow which English farmers began buying at the rate of 700–800 a year because of its enormous yield of high-quality milk. The now familiar fawn-coloured animal with dark muzzle proved the most attractive to buyers and other colours were eventually bred out.

The 1930s saw the popularity of Jersey cattle reaching its highest peak, with a steady 1,000 a year leaving the island. All over the world dairies were boasting that their milk and dairy products were derived from Jersey herds. From the

47

islanders' point of view, the cow possessed the inestimable advantage of deteriorating after a few generations when taken from its native habitat, so that the trade appeared to be self-perpetuating.

Long Jack

Because grazing is possible all the year round in Jersey, cows are to be seen tethered in the fields in winter, often wearing coats made of tarpaulin or sacking to keep them warm and maintain the milk yield. However, as a standby feed for the few days when they could not be put out to graze, a new crop was introduced which came to be regarded as something of a local curiosity. Farmers started to grow small patches of *brassica oleraica longata*, a cabbage brought from La Vendée. Called 'Long Jack' because of its 10–12ft stalks, it not only provided cattle feed but the leaves were used for wrapping the rich, yellow butter for market, and a traditional loaf—the Jersey cabbage loaf—was baked upon them; the stalks made strong, lightweight walking-sticks, once much sought after but now seldom seen.

LIVING FROM THE SEA

In early times, fishing was a local activity, secondary to farming, and the men would return to the land in time for the ploughing. In the fifteenth century John Cabot's discovery of Newfoundland opened up rich new fishing grounds and led to a big expansion in the island's fishery operations. Vessels from Spain, Portugal and Brittany began to exploit this source of supply and Jerseymen probably sailed in Breton boats until they started to voyage there in their own, covering thousands of miles in a year.

In 1666 a pier was built at St Aubin in the west of Jersey at the instigation of the governor, Thomas Morgan. This, the first protected harbour in the island, was capable of taking the

48

largest ships of the Newfoundland fishing fleet, and at the same time offered a haven for foreign vessels.

The Treaty of Utrecht of 1713, which ended the War of the Spanish Succession, gave Jersey a virtual monopoly of the fisheries since the French renounced all claims and the island's boats were able to operate under Royal Navy protection.

Trading

At this period the Jerseymen became not so much fishermen as entrepreneurs. Jersey's ships carried stores, clothing, boots and shoes for sale in Newfoundland and Canada, where along the east coast and particularly on the Gaspé peninsula of Quebec the island's association with the area is recorded in their place names. There they loaded up with salt cod for South America and Spain, to supply the market created by the Catholic feast days, and exchanged it for hides, wine and other goods for home consumption or resale to Britain. The Jerseymen owned many of the fishing stations and island finance was so heavily involved that when one of the Jersey banks failed in 1886 there were riots among the Newfoundland fishermen who demanded the return of the money they had deposited with it.

Smuggling

Elizabeth I and Charles II had each in turn reaffirmed the island's charters which included the privilege of being allowed to import its goods into England without duties—on equal terms with home produce. Jersey had always given the widest possible interpretation to such free-port access. Any attempt by the British to close this loophole resulted in the islanders calling on the world community to witness how their 'ancient rights and charters' were being violated. In this way statutes aimed at preventing the importation of a particular commodity, often to protect the indigenous British trade, could be very simply flouted.

As customs' duties on goods came to be a more important source of revenue to the Treasury, this situation became a matter for concern. In 1681, an exciseman was sent to Jersey to check on the loading and unloading of tobacco cargoes. His task proved to be not only thankless, but dangerous. On arrival, he was seized and set upon by ruffians, and when he tried to start work the island authorities refused any co-operation. With his life in constant danger, the unfortunate man had to be removed and no further attempts at interference were made.

The island continued, as hitherto, to provide a warehouse for contraband of every description. British protestation produced the reply that since someone was certain to practise smuggling, it was better that profits therefrom should accrue to His Majesty's loyal Jersey subjects rather than to aliens or perhaps enemies.

In 1768 George III's government required that all Channel Island vessels should be cleared through a British port. This was not only an infringement of the island charters but, more importantly, threatened the thriving smuggling operations. To fight this ruling, the Jersey Chamber of Commerce was formed —the oldest in the British Isles—and was so successful in its efforts that direct trade was able to resume.

The trade was two-way: it was a question not only of brandy for the parson, but also of whisky for the abbé. Both changed hands as boats from Jersey met those from Normandy or Brittany clandestinely somewhere between the island and the French coast.

It was as a spin-off to smuggling activities that Jersey's wealth of chilling ghost-legends were born. It can hardly have been coincidence that apparitions like the Bouley Bay dog, with its saucer eyes and rattling chains, was said to be encountered at one of the smugglers' principal landing places.

Shipbuilding

Complementary to the sea trade, a shipbuilding industry developed on the island, with yards all along the coast from St Aubin to St Catherine. Within a few years, 450 trading vessels were built and the island's shipping tonnage rose from 9,000 to 50,000. The advent of iron and steel ships driven by steam power led to a decline in the industry, and towards the end of the nineteenth century the yards were being forced to close, one after another.

Privateering

The continental wars of the eighteenth century offered fresh opportunities to the island's privateers. Many captains of the sizeable Jersey merchant fleet applied for letters of marque, fitted swivel guns to their ships and sailed off in search of prey. By the end of the War of the Spanish Succession, there were fifty-one privateers operating out of Jersey and more than twice that number from Guernsey.

As the profits of this activity became greater, bigger ships were employed, some with a displacement of 200 tons and armed with as many as twenty guns. By 1711 Jersey privateers had taken 151 ships, and during the Seven Years' War alone they brought in prize worth £60,000. The American War of Independence, in which France supported the insurgent colonists, saw no fewer than 150 French vessels anchored in St Aubin's Bay and large numbers of French seamen held prisoner in the island.

All this activity was a provocation which the French could not be expected to tolerate for ever, especially when the privateers were not content to stick to the sea, but indulged in land forays also. In one of these, at Caen, oxen, cows, sheep and all the washing of the local curé as well as two of his washerwomen were carried off. One can sympathise with the governor of Cherbourg who was driven to expostulate: 'These islands are the despair of France, at the breaking out of each war, through their remarkably active privateers . . .'

In 1778, £343,500 worth of shipping and goods had been brought in by twenty privateers; the following year £270,000 had been garnered by a mere six, and three years later £156,500 by five. During the Napoleonic Wars the island privateers were less successful. The French vessels were well armed and fast, with the consequence that Jersey lost two-thirds of her ships. Though the rest made rich profits, the defeat of Napoleon and the freeing of the seas brought an end to the island's privateering.

Shellfish

Over the same period, there had been a fresh development in fishery enterprise when oyster beds were laid out at Gorey in the east of the island. This soon developed into a most profitable industry with the local women and girls employed in sorting the oysters brought ashore from the dredgers.

In due course, British-owned ships located the beds, but as supplies were so prolific the islanders did not at first make any attempt to discourage the intruders. Soon, however, the British began to exploit the beds with such ruthless greed and disregard for oyster breeding that there was a danger of their total destruction. As the catches grew smaller, the British lost interest and started dredging the French beds off Chaussey.

The Jerseymen sighed with relief and restocked their beds at a cost of some £40,000—a considerable sum for a small community at that time. But the British, driven off by the French who were not prepared to see their oyster beds depleted as the Jersey ones had been, returned to the island waters. The Jerseymen warned them off, but the British disregarded all threats until the island's militia brought their artillery down to the coast; under their muzzles, the poachers set sail and departed.

Plate 5 St Aubin: (*above*) the sea front; (*below*) the fort, viewed from the water's edge. St Aubin was once the centre of the island's fishing and shipping industries.

Plate 6 (*Above*) Ouaisné Bay in the foreground with St Brelade's Bay in the centre of the picture. This bay with its fine sandy beaches and blue waters is one of the most popular tourist spots in the island; (*below*) La Corbière lighthouse on the south west coast. It was built by the island government in 1873 to mark a spot which, hitherto, had been a death-trap for ships.

The oyster trade continued to flourish and by 1857 was bringing in an annual income of some £50,000, but constant over-dredging eventually killed the industry and by 1864 only twenty-three boats remained. Today, in the east of the island, an occasional friable and bleached shell can still be found lying in the mud at low tide.

It was off the eastern side of Jersey that most of the fishing was done, and in the neighbouring parishes the itinerant fish-monger—often a fisherman's wife pushing her loaded barrow—was once a regular sight. The palatial market in St Helier where fish of every kind, much of it locally caught, was enticingly displayed on white marble among blocks of ice and parsley has now been replaced by a smaller and more modern one nearby. The island's fishing industry dwindled almost to nothing over the centuries, and the few remaining full-time fishermen, and a larger number of part-time ones, directed their attention towards gathering shellfish. Pots of basketware or, more recently, of wood and chicken-wire, are to be seen everywhere at low tide, sometimes containing a few small crabs among the debris of seaweed and, occasionally, the purple-black form of a lobster. The lobsters are bought by local hotels and restaurants, some of whom have built up such a reputation that visitors come from France to sample their excellent quality.

4   GOVERNMENT AND THE LAW

W HATEVER differences of breeding, history, ideology or language might separate the Jerseyman from his European neighbours, he could hardly have survived in independence into the twentieth century but for the vitality of his institutions—some of which, like the parish assemblies and the jurats, antedated and outlived the period of Norman domination.

PARISH ASSEMBLIES

The parish assembly, the extension into modern times of *l'ouie de la paroisse*, probably has its origins in some tribal moot of great antiquity, developed under the Franks. There are twelve such assemblies, and each is headed by a *connétable* or constable. The *salle paroissiale* usually stands near the parish church and the body that meets there levies rates, provides help for the needy, and is responsible for refuse collection.

Its principal representatives are the *procureurs du bien public*, but all payers of *foncier*—ground rate—have a right to attend meetings and vote on issues.

The office of constable is an ancient one, known to pre-date the list going back to 1529 in St Helier town hall. Besides presidency of the parish assembly, the constable possesses an executive arm represented by the centeniers, vingteniers and constable's officers, who all act in an elected, honorary capacity and whose principal responsibility is the policing of the parish.

The centenier had charge of 100 households and the vingtenier twenty—hence the derivation of the names; when Jersey was less populous this applied literally. They knew every family in a parish and were able to resolve quarrels, outbursts of drunken violence and other disturbances of the civil peace with discretion and humanity. They still have power to impose certain summary fines and to hold 'inquiries' into accidents, often settling these matters without the need for court action.

Although a trained police force has existed in Jersey since the 1840s, the centeniers are the senior officers. The professionals were understandably exasperated at being subordinate to men untrained in police work, whose investigative function often led to justifiable criticism. Those who suffered the attention of a criminal would experience difficulties and delays at every stage of the police inquiry, so that the dignity and amour propre of a centenier should not be affronted, even at the cost of failure to apprehend the miscreant. The resident of St Helier was at a considerable advantage over the countrydweller, the rural centenier often being a farmer working in his fields who had to be tracked down when needed.

The situation might seem to savour of farce—as it sometimes did—but crime only became a problem on the island with large-scale immigration; in former days, front doors could be left unlocked without risk while the occupant was in bed or away from home.

In recent years, the ancient honorary police system has twice come under critical scrutiny. The first occasion was in a report prepared by a chief superintendent from Scotland Yard sent over to assist the local CID in its inquiries into a series of sex crimes on the island. The second was in a report from R. G. Fenwick, HM Inspector of Constabulary, after an inspection of the States Police Force in 1971. The first report was kept secret and the second published only in abridged form. The parts omitted were, it was rumoured, those most critical of the honorary system and the deletion demonstrative of their power.

The published extracts certainly had strong things to say, for example: 'Untrained and virtually unaccountable, the honorary police are required by law to take a leading part in the island's police arrangements; in practice, they simply cannot do so, despite valiant attempts to prove otherwise. As time passes, their police function, based on great antiquity and steeped in island traditions, must surely be revealed more as an anachronism and allowed to lapse.'

There is, as yet, no sign of its lapsing. The report was promptly and strongly attacked by the centeniers, who pointed out that the system saved the island something like £250,000 a year in policing. Certainly, the existence of the honorary police does not appear to have reduced the chance of apprehending offenders; where there has been failure in this respect it is more often due to causes endemic to the island than to internal deficiency.

A debate in the States in May 1974 indicated strong opposition to change; the only reform made was that henceforward an honorary police officer, when in pursuit of an offender, would be free to cross parish boundaries—previously he had to abandon the chase while the police of the parish concerned were called out to take over!

THE JURATS

In early times the jurats—in full, the *jurés-justiciers* (sworn justices)—no doubt filled the role of parish or village chieftains. Later they became judges of both fact and law, but from the nineteenth century, when trained practitioners of the law were required, they remained judges of fact only, though still addressed in court as 'the learned jurats'.

The twelve jurats, under the presidency of the bailiff, formed the Royal Court, which administers the island law, both civil and criminal. The Royal Court could be said to have as its foundation some age-old gathering of island elders, who not only deliberated on matters of governance, but also tried offenders and arbitrated in disputes. Thus, the twelve jurats were also the island government.

In the fifteenth century, the need to be aware of local opinion led to the introduction into the Royal Court, in a consultative capacity, of the parish constables and rectors; it was out of this that the Jersey parliament, among the oldest in Europe, came into being. This assembly took the name of 'The States' from the *États*, which were responsible for government at provincial and national level in France.

As the two bodies divided, there was at first some rivalry, but lines of demarcation evolved and the States became the acknowledged legislative authority, though the seniority of the Royal Court is still recognised in its ratification and registration of all Acts of the States—a practice which is now a mere formality.

The States claimed from a very early date to be governing according to the will of the people, though the wishes to which it gave substance were by no means always in accord with those of the Crown-delegated governors of the island.

THE LIEUTENANT-GOVERNOR

The sovereign is represented in Jersey by a lieutenant-governor, a senior officer of high rank, who holds the post for five years. In recognition of the earlier functions of the governor, he is also commander-in-chief, though he has no troops to command.

The last governor to take up his post on the island was Lord Beresford in 1834, by which time the importance of the office

59

had declined as Jersey's strategic role came to an end after the Napoleonic Wars. The long rivalry between governor and bailiff had resulted, in 1618, in a ruling that the bailiff was to take precedence in all courts of justice and in the States Assembly, but elsewhere the governor took first place, 'without further question'.

Today the lieutenant-governor is largely a figurehead. Jersey passports are issued in his name and, under Article 33 of the States of Jersey Law 1966, he has the right to veto any resolution of the States, which merely confirms the position before its incorporation into law. He is also a member of the Assembly of Governor, Bailiff and Jurats—a body comparable to the British licensing bench—but rarely attends sittings.

He is invariably invited to become patron of local societies of standing; he attends the more important island functions—where his position as sovereign's representative is recognised by the playing of the national anthem; he acts as host to visiting royalty and holds a levée on the sovereign's birthday. The lieutenant-governor also advises the Home Secretary on Crown appointments.

THE BAILIFF

In island terms, the highest office is that of bailiff. In recognition of his precedence, as laid down in 1618, the bailiff's chair in the States Chamber and the Royal Court is mounted a few inches higher than the lieutenant-governor's.

The bailiff combines the functions of chief magistrate, speaker of the States and, in some ways, prime minister and foreign secretary—so far as Jersey's dealings with other states are concerned. He presides over the electoral college which appoints jurats, and ratifies the results of local elections. Since he is the sole judge of law in the Royal Court, he must be an advocate.

The office of bailiff is an appointment and not an elected office, and the normal steps towards it are solicitor-general, attorney-general and deputy bailiff. Apart from a deputy, the bailiff is assisted by a number of lieutenant bailiffs, who are jurats. The bailiff is also deputy lieutenant-governor and acts for him when he is absent from the island.

THE STATES

By the middle of the nineteenth century, there was some objection to the fact that, apart from the constables, the States contained no elected representatives. In 1857, following the first 'popular' election, the first deputies—three for St Helier and one for each country parish—took their places in the assembly for a three-year period. The number of town deputies was increased to six in 1907. With the passing of the Reform Acts of 1948, the total of deputies in the States was raised to twenty-eight, and the twelve rectors lost their seats in the assembly.

The jurats too no longer sat in the States; their place was taken by twelve senators elected on an all-island poll. A third of their number stand down every three years so that the maximum period for which a senator holds his seat without re-election is nine years. Besides giving a body of experienced men to the assembly, the longer period of service aimed at achieving continuity of government.

From 1948 the constitution of the States thus became: 12 constables, 12 senators, 28 deputies—52 in all. The attorney-general, the solicitor-general and the Dean of Jersey each had a seat and were permitted to address the assembly, but had no vote.

The States is divided into a number of standing committees, each under a president. It is the discussion and acceptance or rejection of the recommendations of these committees, as well as the enactment of legislation presented through them, that forms the corpus of States' business. Though the States is competent to pass laws, these do not become enforceable until they have received the royal assent. Acts go through a process of three readings and in their initial stages are 'lodged *au greffe*'—that is, placed with the Clerk of the House—at which time they are available to public scrutiny.

The House does not divide on contentious issues, but there may be a call for an *appel nominal* in which each member records his '*pour*' or '*contre*' as his name is called out by the *greffier*. These few words are among the sole remnants of the French in which, until 1899, the business of the House was transacted; another example is the prayers which open sittings. The States normally meets weekly for a one-day session, nowadays held in the special chamber completed in 1887.

Party politics

In the eighteenth century, the burgeoning of radical and populist movements had its repercussions in Jersey, where a group—nicknamed the 'Magots' (maggots)—was formed to break the grip of the powerful seigneurial côterie, which held on to the island's principal offices as of hereditary right. Their opponents, led by the bailiff, Charles Lemprière, came to be known as the 'Charlots'. The Magot leader, Jean Dumaresq, a man grounded in the ideas of the French *philosophes*, Benjamin Franklin, Tom Paine and the 'Rights of Man', gained a majority for his party in the States in 1781; by 1790 it also had a majority among the jurats.

There was a further recrudesence of party politics after the Napoleonic Wars, with the Progressives, who took the rose as their emblem, and the Conservatives, who took for theirs the laurel leaf, as contenders. Party hatred reached such bitterness that it was said to be dangerous to present a bouquet of roses to a woman or to place a laurel sprig in her hair, lest she be of the other faction. 'It is utterly impossible,' wrote Henry D. Inglis, 'for anyone unaquainted with Jersey to form any idea of the lengths to which party spirit is carried there. It not only taints the fountains of public justice, but enters into the most private relations of life.'

Today's absence of party politics is often held up as a merit in the system as avoiding the dissensions of partisanship. Although to some extent true, in practice it means the island has no government with an agreed programme for which the electorate have given it a mandate. The consequence is a declining interest in government, as reflected by low polls. Increasingly large numbers of islanders feel their wishes are never consulted or, if they are, cannot by the nature of the system be taken into account. There is a certain amount of trading in votes as one president will offer those of his own committee to get a measure through the House in return for those of another on some future issue. The end result is that States' members are seen—not altogether fairly—as the managers of an enterprise, rather than as the elected representatives of the people carrying out their chosen policies.

Members' allowances

There has recently been some public debate on the subject of outside financial interests of States' members, although it is impossible to control these in an assembly whose members serve in a voluntary capacity. Wild accusations are made from time to time but there has never been any solid evidence that members of the States gain personal benefit from their situation. On the other hand, it is sometimes pointed out that, being voluntary, membership is restricted to those who have the necessary time available and who accordingly are to be numbered among the better off. To try to correct this, in December 1969, expenses up to a maximum of £750 were paid to members whose incomes did not exceed £1,500 a year; in 1972 this allowance was increased to £1,000 and in 1974 to £1,500. Even this has not entirely satisfied opposition groups

63

who claim that States' work, when committee meetings and other functions are included, can take up four days a week.

Policy Advisory Committee

Although the traditional States' system of rule by committee continues, a so-called Policy Advisory Committee has been established; this is a co-ordinating body with the presidents of the most important committees as its members. One of its first tasks has been to lay down economic guidelines for the next five years, taking into consideration such matters as the inter-relation of rising standards of living and the need to safeguard the environment. Their deliberations resulted in the publication in 1974 of *The Pattern for Development*, more properly the *Report and Proposition Regarding the Scale and Pattern of Development in the Island Over the Next Five Years*. The PAC has come in for some attack. There are those who feel that this is introducing Cabinet rule; it is seen as the concentration of power into a few hands and, as such, a move away from open democracy.

'Ombudsman Tribunal'

As a counterbalance to the increased bureaucracy that has grown up in the island, the States has established the Administrative Decisions (Review) (Jersey) Regulation. This has brought into being a review body, popularly called the 'Ombudsman Tribunal', through which complaints against governmental decisions can be heard. Each of the States' committee presidents sits in turn on the panel.

THE LEGAL SYSTEM

The foundation of much local law is the *Le Grand Coutumier de Normandie*, a summary of Norman law published in 1199. One custom still retained in the island, coming from the *Grand Cou-*

tumier, is that of *Clameur de Haro,* which gives direct access to the courts. Under this anyone who feels himself wronged may, by going down on his knees and shouting '*Haro, haro, haro! à l'aide, mon Prince. On me fait tort*' before two witnesses, bring about the immediate cessation of the offending act. This injunction continues until the case has been heard by a court.

Certain elements of local law, as they developed, were encapsulated in the so-called *Code of 1771* which, among other things, laid down permissible rates of interest and was to be of considerable importance to the island.

Taken as a whole, however, Jersey law is English Common Law, with the statutes of the States superadded. Occasionally an English law will be copied, adapted or extended to the island—as happened, for example, with the British Independent Television Act when independent television was brought to the Channel Islands.

The process of anglicisation has spread into the legal system more and more. Where a few decades ago the island advocates —who combine the functions of barristers and solicitors—were trained in the University of Caen, in Normandy, and spoke French, now they are British trained. English precedents are those most often cited and English is used in pleadings.

Court procedure

Both States Chamber and Royal Court are housed in a row of somewhat bleak buildings along one side of Royal Square, St Helier, once also the market place. In a large room, overpoweringly gloomy despite its picture-hung walls, all but one of the island's courts meet. The court has its own officers: the attorney-general, solicitor-general and Crown solicitor, who are appointed to their posts and act on behalf of the Crown and States in all civil, criminal and mixed causes, besides guiding the States in matters of law. There is also an executive law officer attached to the court who bears the title of viscount—

or *vicomte*—and whose function is much like that of a tipstaff or bailiff.

In the court the lieutenant-governor, when he attends, wears a red cloak over his service uniform. The bailiff, attorney-general, solicitor-general and jurats wear red robes trimmed with black velvet. No wigs or headgear are worn.

The Royal Court

The Royal Court sits under two heads: as the Inferior Number, in which the bailiff is supported by two jurats; or as the Full Court, in which he is supported by not less than seven and sometimes all twelve. The Inferior Number has unlimited adjudication as to fact, but is restricted in the punishment it can inflict. Thus, a defendant may be found guilty of serious crimes by the Inferior Number, but must go before the Full Court, which can impose even capital punishment, for sentence.

There were obvious objections to a form of justice in which it could be said that a man, faced by a bench of jurats, was not being tried by his peers. By a law of 1864 a Court of Assize was therefore introduced. This includes a jury of twenty-four persons and the assent of two-thirds is necessary to secure a finding of guilt. The law prohibits the trial of cases, save in matters of high treason, out of the island; so that, where a case is contentious or where high emotions are involved, a defendant may proffer reasons for wishing to be tried by the Royal Court. The right to grant the request lies with the court.

The Royal Court also acts as a civil court and certain contracts, such as those involving property or land sales or the formation of new companies, have to be registered before it.

All prosecutions in the Royal Court are carried out either by the attorney-general or by the solicitor-general. If the defendant is found guilty, the prosecution also makes submissions as to sentence, except in cases like murder where a mandatory sentence is involved. While the bailiff is sole judge of law in the Royal Court, the jurats determine sentence at Assize sittings and, in civil cases, assess damages.

In the past, appeals against Royal Court judgements were heard by the legal committee of the Privy Council; now they are heard by a bench of three judges sent from Britain when they are needed.

Assise d'Heritage

Unique to the islands, and claiming to be the oldest land court in Europe, it meets twice a year for the purpose of allowing seigneurs and fiefs of the island's manors to renew their fealty.

Ecclesiastical court

Early in the reign of Richard II (1377–99), the Bishop of Coutances summoned a number of islanders to appear before him. They refused on the ground that they could not be tried outside their own island. The bishop then formed a local court of deans, for ecclesiastical cases, which in practice often clashed with the Royal Court. Today, it is made up of the Dean of Jersey, who is president, and eleven assessors, who are rectors of the other parishes and from whose number the dean appoints two vice-deans. The court deals with ecclesiastical business of all kinds, though it has lost its probate jurisdiction.

Police courts

The Police Court and Petty Debts Courts meet in a room in St Helier Town Hall. The police court adjudicates on minor cases, such as traffic infractions or small-scale larcenies, and also hears the committal evidence in more serious ones. It is presided over by a stipendiary magistrate; the presence of such a trained lawyer is necessary because of the court's form and procedure. There is, for example, no prosecutor. Cases are actually 'presented' by the centenier in whose area an offence

67

has taken place. 'Presentation' means no more than the bringing together of witnesses and the organisation of evidence. In the actual context of the hearing, the centenier is simply a witness, though he is allowed, in order to offer an overall initial picture, to make use of hearsay evidence, such as what a complainant told him when he arrived on the scene of a crime.

Defendants before this court, even where their cases are destined to be heard by a higher one, may be represented by an advocate, who may cross-examine, plead for his client or submit that no prima facie case has been made out.

With a layman on the prosecution side opposed by a lawyer on the defence side, the magistrate must seek to drive a path between them to arrive at the truth. He is, therefore, more akin to the *juge d'instruction* of a Continental court than to a Justice of the Peace in England.

Proposed changes in judicature

A Special Committee, presided over by the attorney-general, which reported in 1974, made a series of recommendations: the number of jurors in the Assize Court should, it thought, be reduced from the present twenty-four to twelve, with a majority of nine (three-quarters) instead of the present sixteen (two-thirds) necessary for conviction, and the number of jurats sitting at an assize should be reduced from seven to five. At the same time the number sitting with the bailiff in the Inferior Number of the Royal Court should be increased from two to three; this is to obviate the need, in case of disagreement, for the bailiff to use his casting vote, which traditionally went in favour of the accused.

The committee further recommended that the bailiff should sum-up in open court, as happened in a recent case, and not to the jurats alone, as was done hitherto.

It also recommended that, while prosecutions in the Royal Court should continue to be conducted by the attorney-general or the solicitor-general, thought should be given to establishing a panel of prosecuting advocates for the magistrates' court, inaugurating the adversary system there.

At present a defendant may apply to the arresting centenier for bail; if the committee's recommendations are adopted he would, where this is refused, be given a statutory right of appeal to a jurat or magistrate.

5 THE OCCUPATION AND AFTER

THE outbreak of war in September 1939 at first had little effect on Jersey. As in World War I, young islanders left to join the British forces and again the militia was mobilised, but so remote from the struggle was the island thought to be that, to the fury of some local people, a party of conscientious objectors was sent over to work on the farms. In the British newspapers, Jersey advertised itself as 'the ideal resort for wartime holidays'.

This smug picture was shattered in May 1940 by the German *Blitzkrieg*. The island's initial brush with the realities of war came when every available small boat was sent to assist in the evacuation of St Malo, and it was the sight of the demoralised French and British troops, many without their weapons, which struck the first chill of apprehension into the islanders.

In mid-June the Admiralty warned that, if France fell, the Channel Islands would be indefensible; and, with the French capitulation, the British government agreed to their demilitarisation. Lieutenant-governors and troops departed, and shipping was provided for those islanders who wished to follow them. The awareness of German forces just across the sea and the feeling of abandonment resulted in a panic in which 10,000 men and women from Jersey rushed to seek refuge in a country unfamiliar to them, some uprooting themselves from the land their families had tilled for centuries, even leaving their cattle in the fields.

Plate 7 St Ouen: the manor, for more than eight hundred years the home of the de Carteret family

Plate 8 Plémont Bay on the north coast, facing out toward the Atlantic, is a popular spot for surfing and the high cliffs which overhang it are honeycombed with caves

In late June, with all defences removed, the islands were bombed and strafed in what was perhaps the first move towards a German attack. The actions were sporadic and small-scale, but the marauding aircraft, unopposed and causing a disproportionate number of casualties, prompted a feeling of desperation.

By 1 July it must have become plain to the enemy that Jersey was no longer defended. The Germans dropped an ultimatum demanding orderly and peaceful surrender and the island government responded in the only way possible. That day Alexander Coutanche, the bailiff, addressed a crowd in St Helier's Royal Square, explaining what was happening and urging that they keep calm and obeyed the occupiers' orders. 'I do not know when I shall have the opportunity of speaking to you again,' he concluded, 'but until then I pray God's blessing upon you all.'

WARTIME LEADERSHIP

Alexander Moncrieff Coutanche was the descendant of an old Jersey family, having Robert the Bruce among his ancestors. An advocate, he was returned to the States in 1922 as one of the town deputies; three years later he became solicitor-general and, in 1931, attorney-general. When, in 1935, he was appointed bailiff, he determined to fulfil three aims: to open up and maintain a rapport with the Home Office—the Whitehall department responsible for relations with the island; to remain constantly approachable to his fellow islanders—he boasted that his office door was always open and this was true—and to do what he could to bring Jersey into the modern world. He sought to encourage rather than to impose the changes he believed necessary and, in the years before the war, had been very largely responsible for the drive to extend and improve the services and amenities of the island.

Tall, dark, beetle-browed, with a personality which attracted

E

attention the moment he entered a room, Coutanche had something of the air of the old-time actor-manager—larger, and a little noisier, than life. A charming man, an amusing raconteur with a wealth of local anecdote, he was a dedicated democrat who presided impartially over the States, and in the Royal Court gained an international reputation as a jurist.

While he was speaking to the islanders on that July day, the Germans were already beginning to arrive at the airport. For days afterwards, the black Junkers 52 transport planes flew in, one after another, bringing the occupation troops.

The island was placed under the command of a Captain Gussek and the States given limited freedom to carry on as best it could. The Germans had no wish to add to their burdens those of administration and the day-to-day operation of community services which were necessary to them as well. Coutanche and his immediate associates decided on a policy of putting their own people first and doing everything they could to prevent any actions likely to antagonise the Germans, which might persuade them to take over the reins themselves. This fully accorded with the British view, since resistance and the dire consequences that might result could be of considerable embarrassment to Britain and bring it under pressure to relieve the islanders' situation.

This policy naturally caused a certain amount of ill-feeling among those islanders who longed to do something to help the war effort. On the other hand it meant that interposed between the Germans and themselves was a government of their fellows, able to do at least something to mitigate their lot.

UNDER GERMAN CONTROL

In overall command of the Channel Islands was a veteran of the regular German army, General Count Rudolf von Schmettow. An unquestioning and loyal soldier who had held a corps command on the Eastern Front in World War I, he so hated the excesses of the Nazis that throughout the war refugee Jews were given sanctuary on his Silesian farm. In so far as he was able, he was determined to spare the islanders the worst rigours of occupation and, among other things, successfully kept the Gestapo and SS units from any of the islands.

1940–4

The occupying troops behaved impeccably and for the first few weeks the worst ordeal the people suffered was to watch the German planes massing overhead on their way to carry out raids on England. By the end of August, however, relations were turning sour. Familiarity was breeding a dangerous contempt among Jerseymen, a people accustomed to independence. The imposition of a curfew and other restrictions chafed badly. Supplies were beginning to run short and purchasing missions were sent to France to try to secure at least some essentials. The farmers were turning from their normal potato and tomato crops to wheat, but it would be a year before the first harvest. Meanwhile a thriving barter trade developed between the farmers, who could supply some of the necessities and even a few of the luxuries of life, and the rest of the islanders.

In the aftermath of the Battle of Britain, feeling themselves in a backwater of the war, the people suffered the consequences of boredom and frustration. The chalking up of V-signs and the cutting of telegraph wires led to reprisals, which von Schmettow sought in some degree to mitigate, not always successfully; many people were sent to German political prisons and some ended their lives in the concentration camps.

Coutanche protested constantly about the increasing shortage of food and other necessities. His relations with the occupying authorities were correct though not cordial. The Germans were secretly not unsympathetic to the situation and respected his courage, but there was little they could do. As the months

75

rolled by, the position of the islanders became more difficult and they adopted an ingenious variety of substitutes for those commodities no longer available. Flour was made from potatoes, and a species of sweetening syrup from sugarbeet; blackberry leaves, lime flowers, rose leaves, carrots and pea pods became an alternative to tea, and roast parsnips, swedes and acorns were used instead of coffee. As a substitute for tobacco, all manner of hedgerow seeds were smoked in pipes, and in cigarettes which were rolled from any sort of paper that could be found.

In 1941 the Channel Islands found themselves once more fulfilling the historical role of outpost as Hitler built up his defences in western Europe, following his invasion of Russia. To build the concrete bunkers, gun-emplacements and watchtowers, 18,000 slave-workers were brought to Jersey. They included Spanish refugees from the Franco regime, caught in France by the occupation, Frenchmen, Belgians and Dutchmen. Most ill-fated of all were the Russian prisoners of war. They had been marched across Europe under the control of whip-cracking labour overseers of the Todt Organisation, and uncounted thousands of men, women and children had died on the journey. The Russian p.o.w.'s, dehumanised by suffering and hunger, were housed in camps bare of the most fundamental amenities. The people of Jersey living near by were kept awake by night-long screaming. Thousands died or were killed. A few escaped and the luckier ones found sanctuary in island homes. Some were successfully hidden away, but others were discovered or denounced and, together with the people who had given them refuge, were sent to concentration camps where many of them died.

In September 1942 some 1,200 British-born residents were ordered to be deported from the island to Germany, where Hitler planned to use them as hostages to prevent allied bombing of German cities. Schmettow questioned the order, but as it had originated from the Führer himself he could do nothing to prevent it being carried out. The Germans directed the constables and parish authorities to draw up lists of those who were to go and to warn them they must be ready to leave at twenty-four hours' notice. Appalled by this inhumanity, the constables' first inclination was to refuse categorically at no matter what cost. On reconsideration, however, it was decided that there was something to be said for at least the appearance of co-operation. The presentation of a deportation order to a family by a local man would help to cushion the shock. By passive resistance and an intentional misunderstanding of instructions, they were able to bring about delays and to serve the orders on people known to the constable to be sick or over seventy, though the Germans had expressly excluded these two categories.

Because of what appeared to the ordinary people as overzealousness in carrying out their masters' bidding, the parish authorities earned much opprobrium; had they refused compliance, however, the Germans would have carried out the whole scheme themselves with the maximum efficiency. As it was, the machinery set up for the deportation became so clogged that in the end the whole enterprise was brought to an early end.

On top of all this, the island government had to make clear to its people that it could do nothing to help those who wittingly antagonised the occupiers through acts of sabotage; this only added to the notion of collaboration with the enemy, although when people were caught, appeals for clemency were made secretly on their behalf.

The Germans, on the other hand, were under no similar constraints and were only too happy to present themselves as the benefactors of the people whose island they were occupying. Often, therefore, it was made to look as if they and not the Jerseymen of the government had islanders' interests at heart.

The net result was a seething discontent against the island leadership. There was a feeling among the public that their rulers had totally betrayed their trust, and this expressed itself through the formation of a political party—the Jersey Democratic Party—in the latter days of the occupation. Collecting round it various radical elements, it sought a full inquiry into the island government's conduct of affairs and, assuming that this would show them to be guilty of heinous failures, wanted the island to become a British county, returning a Member to the House of Commons. Officially, the party's organisation was carried out in secret as political parties were prohibited from operating, but the Germans, who knew of it, were prepared to turn a blind eye since it embarrassed the island government.

1944–5

Following the allied invasion of Normandy, some 36,000 German troops were isolated in the Channel Islands, because of what the German general staff called 'Hitler's Island madness'—his refusal to surrender the one tiny corner of British territory in his hands. In June 1944, Admiral Hüffmeier, former commander of the *Scharnhorst*, arrived in Jersey, having escaped when the French island of Cézembre fell to the allies. A rabid Nazi, he persuaded his superiors in Germany that he should take overall command of the Channel Islands, to defend them 'to the last man'. Schmettow was duly recalled and, under their new overlord, the islanders entered the last and worst phase of occupation.

Life was now at its lowest ebb. The islanders were thin, hungry, ill-clothed, tired. After the liberation of Normandy, they had confidently expected that allied forces would be sent to free them, but by the winter it was certain this was not to be. The islands were of no strategic value to the allies and for them to try and take these heavily defended fortresses by a

78

coup de main would have been to risk enormous casualties, not least among the civilian population themselves. To the people of Jersey even the possibility of death in a violent bid for liberation seemed preferable to being starved into surrender.

Some efforts had been made to contact the Red Cross to ask for food, but these had encountered the objections of Winston Churchill, who felt that, if supplies reached the civilians in the islands, the Germans—being themselves short of food now that the fitful supply lines on the French mainland had been cut off—would no doubt take the remaining stocks and thus be given a fresh lease of life. The Germans must feed the islanders, and if they did not then the people must face a patriotic death from starvation. Churchill's colleagues finally persuaded him that these were British subjects who were being sacrificed at this late stage in the war, and in mid-November he gave in. On 7 December the Red Cross ship *Vega* left Lisbon carrying food parcels and other supplies, arriving in the islands a few days after Christmas. There was an immediate distribution of parcels and the remainder were put into store for a further hand-out in a month's time. It is to the credit of the German army, which provided guards for the warehouse that, despite the soldiers' own hunger, not a single parcel was touched.

By January 1945, however, the people's daily ration was only ¼oz meat, 10z of breakfast meal, 100z of bread, ¼oz of butter, ½pt of milk, ½lb of potatoes—nothing else. There was no sugar, no salt, and butter was rapidly running out. There was no coal, coke or wood fuel. Medical supplies, including anaesthetics, were nearly exhausted.

Coutanche addressed a sternly worded protest to the occupying authorities reminding them of their duties under international law. Since they were no longer able to fulfil these obligations, their occupation should, he declared, be brought to an end. He closed ominously with the warning that the day would come when the powers would come together to pass judgement on those who had determined the fates of occupied peoples. 'May the Insular Government be spared the duty of adding to the problems which will face the Powers an allegation that . . . the Military Representatives of the German Government unnecessarily endangered the health and indeed the lives of the people of Jersey.' The protest was duly passed on to the German government through a neutral 'protecting power', but nothing was done.

It was felt that if only details of the position could be conveyed to London something would be done to help. In fact, a local fisherman carrying a dossier of statistics had left Guernsey and succeeded in reaching liberated France, but his efforts produced no assistance. Coutanche, with typical flamboyance, suggested that he himself should go to England by yacht under flag of truce and put the situation directly to Westminster; he was almost successful in persuading the German command that the scheme was feasible.

If the position of the civilian population was bad, that of the occupiers was no better. Discontent in the local Wehrmacht units was reaching such a pitch that an attempt was made that winter to assassinate the commandant and his staff. A bomb was planted in one of the island's hotels where Hüffmeier was to attend a meeting; this was postponed, but the fuse mechanism had already been set. It was thus only by a lucky chance that Hüffmeier escaped the enormous explosion which shook the whole eastern half of the island and reduced the hotel to rubble, killing an unknown number of people.

On 8 May came the German surrender. That day the *Vega* arrived in St Helier harbour, bringing some immediate relief, and political prisoners had already been released from the island's gaol. Although ships carrying the liberation forces were anchored in the roadsteads, Hüffmeier refused to acknowledge Germany's capitulation and proclaimed his determination to go on resisting—because, it was said, he hoped to use the islands as a bargaining counter in a peace conference.

By the following day the combined appeals of the local authorities and his own officers led him to reconsider his decision. The German army of occupation, war-weary and on the verge of mutiny, wanted only to strip off their uniforms and go home. At first, under his orders, Hüffmeier's delegates tried to negotiate. They were told there was no opening for talks and the islands had to be surrendered. Realising the impossibility of their position, they accepted. That afternoon British troops—including men of what had been the Jersey Militia, now incorporated into the Hampshire Regiment—began coming ashore.

The ordeal was over. It only remained to count the cost.

THE AFTERMATH

After the first heady days of liberation, there were immediate problems to be faced. Thousands of Germans, now prisoners of war, were still in the island waiting to be sent home. The sorry few Russian slave workers who had survived were also being repatriated—not to their own homes, but to Stalin's labour camps; all had been in contact with the West and that was enough to decree their elimination—even those who had displayed courage and loyalty by escaping were not spared, as was revealed in letters smuggled back to Jersey.

Men demobilised from the forces and families who had left the island in June 1940 were beginning to return—all speaking highly of the hospitality and kindness extended to them in Britain—and they needed houses and jobs.

There remained the physical relics of the war: bunkers and gun emplacements of the Atlantic Wall along the coast and, farther inland, strongpoints built of concrete; in addition there were the guns themselves, with thousands upon thousands of rounds of ammunition to be disposed of. Many hotels had been used as billets or converted to other uses and must be restored before the island's tourist industry could be revived, and roads damaged by years of heavy military traffic needed to be repaired.

Recriminations

Shortly after the liberation, Coutanche's stewardship was recognised when he was awarded a knighthood, but many of those who risked life and liberty on behalf of their fellow islanders during the occupation went unrewarded. Dissatisfaction with the government remained in evidence and there was a call for a commission of inquiry to examine the conduct of those who had collaborated with the Germans, acted as informers or made profits in the Black Market. When neither the local nor the British government would countenance what might have become a campaign of recrimination, this was taken as an admission of guilt in high places. On the whole, States' members would have had nothing to fear, but for many of them, like Coutanche, the occupation had placed them in a peculiarily ambiguous position. Much of what he achieved had to be done in secret. He could hardly announce to the islanders, for example, that he had arranged for a letter with details of their plight to be smuggled into Britain. Even a protest had to be registered discreetly or the enemy recipient might feel he was being put into an impossible position. Many of his protests had in fact been successful and this was largely due to this discretion. But the islanders, knowing nothing of this, believed their leaders to have been supine and craven. Churchill himself, placed in an intolerable dilemma over the Channel Islands in 1944, never forgave Coutanche for his actions; he swore he would never visit Jersey as long as he was bailiff and turned down numerous pressing invitations to do so.

By the end of the occupation there had been growing support for the newly formed Jersey Democratic Party, but in the event, faced by the reality of sacrificing the independence they had so long possessed, the islanders wisely jibbed. In elections for the Jersey States held just after the war only one of its candidates was returned. The more successful group was one which emerged just before the election itself and was comprised largely of local businessmen. Calling itself the Jersey Progressive Party, it stood on a platform of radical conservatism. However, once in the House, party loyalties were very quickly forgotten and the JPP soon ceased to exist.

Nevertheless, the dissatisfactions which had led to the formation of the Jersey Democratic Party, and to its high initial recruitment of members, pointed to deeply rooted grievances. Many of these had existed before the occupation, which simply brought them to a head. In consequence, in 1946, a committee of the Privy Council, headed by Lord Samuel, came to the islands to collect evidence and in due course put forward recommendations for a number of far-reaching reforms.

Readjustment

The occupation had, of course, had deep effects upon the island's finances and economy. A shortage of coinage had led to money being printed locally and the introduction of worthless occupation scrip. There had been no exports, visible or invisible, for five years and so no inflow of cash. Towards the solution of these particular problems the British government offered speedy, efficient and generous assistance, sending a team of financial and economic advisers to give guidance; making a large grant to redeem the occupation *Reichsmarks*, and low interest loans to meet other debts. The island itself had taken steps towards self-help in 1940 by raising income tax, 'as a temporary measure', from $2\frac{1}{2}$p in the £ to 20p, and also increasing duties on tobacco and alcohol. To a Jerseyman the

83

tax increase was astronomical and he saw it as part of the cost of occupation.

The energy which the island threw into the effort of restoring itself could well have served as an object lesson. Home Office doctors investigated the state of the people's health and found it much better than had been expected, and paid tribute to the measures taken to safeguard it during the war years. In some ways it was as if the occupation had never been. Treated as an export market by British manufacturers, the island shops were soon full of goods and there was little shortage of food.

By the summer of 1946, while ground still had to be made up, there was a feeling of normality re-established. The farms, which had been growing wheat, reverted to potatoes and tomatoes. The cattle trade enjoyed a boom as owners of Jersey cows all over the world sought to replenish their herds. British tourists began to return and blinked dazedly in this cornucopian island, so that, by 1948, the holiday industry was on the brink of a boom.

The island now became a haven not merely for those whose incomes had been diminished by retirement, but also for the very wealthy who had a heavy tax burden to bear in Britain. The presence of these new settlers was encouraged, since they were obviously a financial advantage to Jersey, and they began to arrive in increasing numbers during the 1950s. Both they and the tourists, hitherto largely confined to coast and town, were spreading all over the island. The old Jersey manors and the more picturesque farmhouses found ready buyers among the immigrants and hoteliers. The Jerseyman saw his old home become a miniature country estate, with improved façade, landscaped garden and swimming-pool, and any available cottage providing accommodation for the domestic staff the new residents brought with them; or he watched it being transmogrified into a hotel with added wings, and neon lighting to advertise its presence. More and more, the islander was forced

84

into second-class housing: small, ugly boxes on estates, or bungalows built on a corner of land kept back for the purpose from the sale of his property.

Jersey had to come to terms with radically changed attitudes among its own people. Before the war, a high proportion of them never left the island, but in 1940 many had been evacuated and a large number of young men had travelled widely in the services. They were not content now to return to being farm drudges on wages which were poor even by comparison with their counterparts elsewhere. The rising generation wanted equality in education and in job and salary opportunities. An increasingly militant and organised workforce was making its demands known and often gaining them, particularly in those spheres in which postwar growth was leading to a competition for available labour.

Economic recovery

The very nature of the postwar situation dictated economic changes affecting the root and branch of island life. The population had risen by 1951 to 57,296 and local services of all kinds were under pressure. Before the war neither gas nor electricity covered the whole island; water reservoirs were insufficient, especially in a dry summer, and would have been totally inadequate but for the numerous wells and springs still in use. There was a need for an extension of education, housing, medical and hospital services, sewage and refuse disposal, public transport, roads and even policing. Wherever one looked money in vast sums was required; it could only come out of prosperity. Jersey's survival equipment was what it had always been: land, sea, climate. On these the major industries of farming, fishing and tourism had been based; the island now had to turn to them once more and, with whatever other advantages it could give itself, make them supply its needs and provide a big programme of capital investment. Some of the necessary finance could be met from private capital, but not all. The problem was a lack of sources of public revenue. The island had set its face against deficit financing as likely to lead to the sort of internal debt which placed such a burden on Britain.

Money for both capital projects and for day-to-day running of services had therefore to come from the public revenues. These included income tax, harbour and airport dues and some expenditure taxes, mostly in the form of excise duties on wines, spirits, tobacco and petrol. There were no taxes on capital and no death duties, although there was a small, so-called 'company tax', amounting to a fee payable upon registration. Yet there was little room for manoeuvre in these things. Low income tax attracted wealthy residents who, even at a standard rate of 20 per cent, paid enormous sums into the local treasury. Harbour and airport dues could be raised, but not so much as to affect the cost of travel to the island or this would hit tourism; nor must they lead to an increase in the cost of goods brought in to a place that was entirely dependent on imports. Cheap drink, cigarettes and petrol were also a tourist attraction so that duty charged on them had to be kept in proportion to increases elsewhere.

The island had to be mindful of the fact that there were still places where tax levels were lower or, in some instances, nonexistent. Any sharp rise in local taxes could, therefore, result in a flight of capital. The only way Jersey could increase its income from taxes was by bringing in more wealth; this premise formed the basis of all island economic planning and the government founded its policies on encouragement rather than restraint with this in mind.

However, in the very matter of private capital the *Code of 1771* laid down that rates of interest locally must not exceed 5 per cent; even British banks operating in the island were bound by this. There was no problem during the period in which the bank rate stood well below this figure, but once it rose above it local investment was likely to appear unattractive.

As it happened, a chance loophole in British law provided at least a temporary solution. It was discovered that, while money possessed by a British resident of the UK and invested in funds abroad was liable to death duty, there was an exception in the case of money lent on property mortgage. Once this fact had been assimilated in London, there was a rush of capital to Jersey in the late 1950s; with its political and economic stability, it was particularly well-placed to attract it. The lenders were not interested in return so much as in keeping their money at their demise out of the hands of the Department of Inland Revenue. Interest rates dropped lower and lower as funds queued to get into the island. It provided a rich source for hotel purchase or building at a time when much expansion was needed. Indirectly it provided other capital as well, for it was only the original sum which had to be lent for property mortgage and interest rates were often so low that it paid a man to mortgage his home, then reinvest the money.

By 1960 the inflow of money became what the President of the Finance Committee, Senator Cyril Le Marquand, called an '*embarras de richesse*'. Local advocates, who made fortunes out of conveyancing or on the commissions charged on the placement of the loans, advised would-be borrowers not even to worry about interest repayments—they could simply borrow more to pay them! Their main complaint became that often people were too modest in their demands.

It was obviously not a situation which could continue unchecked. Sooner or later, the British government would take action to stem a leak which was rapidly becoming a flood. There was anxiety that the island might come to depend for all its financing upon this rather dubious source so that its loss would precipitate an economic crisis. To the fury of many

87

people in the island, the President of the Finance Committee actually urged upon the British Treasury the need to take this action, which it did in 1961. As something of quid pro quo, however, the sections of the *Code of 1771* on rates of interest were repealed and from then on island rates were tied to the general British bank rate. While the island still possessed its taxation advantages, this it could be said had put its financing on a more realistic basis.

Plate 9 (*above*) Bouley Bay harbour, once a great smuggling centre because of the proximity of the French coast; (*below*) Gorey harbour, with Mont Orgueil castle in the background. The castle guarded the approaches from France which can be seen on a clear day only fifteen miles away.

Plate 10 La Hougue Bie. The picture shows the chapel (actually two joined together) atop the prehistoric tumulus. This was opened in 1924 and what is regarded as one of the finest prehistoric tombs in Europe found within.

6   *TAX HAVEN AND BANKING*
CENTRE

IT was in the early 1960s that the term 'offshore tax haven'
came to be applied to Jersey in British financial circles.
The repeal of the *Code of 1771* and the liberalisation of local
interest rates opened not one but two doors: it invited the rich
to come and live in the island and it encouraged a flow of
money into it. Jersey had as many advantages for money as
for people: it was politically stable, it was in the sterling area
and it was within easy reach of the City of London.

Between 1961 and 1971 the population rose from 62,500 to
72,300—of this increased number, 6,400 were immigrants.
Over the same period the number of motor vehicles on the
island—already abnormally high—went up by 16,000. The
money taken in taxes between 1962 and 1972 increased by
121 per cent in real money, that is, after the drop in values
has been discounted; of this increase 36 per cent came from
taxes on wealthy immigrants. In 1961 States revenues from income taxes, customs and import duties amounted to £3,856,761.
By 1966 it was up to £10,400,870, of which income tax contributed £4,187,772. By 1970 it had reached £11,364,517, with
income tax providing £7,558,580.

IMMIGRANT WEALTH

This rise becomes comprehensible when it is realised that there
are 1,000 people in Jersey whose combined income is around

£10 million and whose tax liability stands at something like £2 million. Of the various sectors of the community paying taxes in 1969 investment holders—in other words, wealthy immigrants—contributed something over a fifth. By 1972 this had risen to nearly a third. The £3 million collected from investment incomes covered the entire expenditure of the States Education Committee that year and could be said to have paid for the running of all the island's primary and secondary schools, and its General Hospital besides.

Very soon after the start of the influx it became obvious that totally free immigration would create fresh problems. The newcomers might be massive contributors to the public purse, but they made other demands. They placed pressure on the labour market; their property purchases could affect the price of agricultural land; they and the not inconsiderable personal staffs they often brought with them used island services of all kinds and, in particular, they were putting extreme pressure on housing resources, thereby giving rise to much local indignation.

It was decided that no house under £10,000 could be sold to a newcomer without the express permission of the States Housing Committee and this ceiling was progressively raised. It was additionally ruled that all property deals, irrespective of price, would need Housing Committee approval. Nevertheless, the flow continued at something in the region of a thousand newcomers a year, even when the minimum for which a house, and a modest one at that, could be bought was £50,000. A new condition was added: the would-be settler must have a local tax liability of at least £10,000 a year, which at a rate of tax of 20p in the £ meant an income of £50,000 a year. This measure not only failed to stem the tide of immigration, but also left the island open to the accusation of being interested only in material considerations.

To control the use of building resources by immigrants,

many of whom have carried out extensions to their new homes costing as much as the original purchase price, regulations introduced in January 1974 made it necessary to have a separate permit for building and development, in addition to planning permission; and it is forbidden for any settler to extend his property by more than 500sq ft in his first year of occupancy.

Conditions of entry

The current situation is that all intending immigrants must apply for permission to settle in the island and their applications are considered on general merit—among the criteria being that of 'social desirability'. In April 1974 it was decided that, of those applicants able to satisfy the island authorities, only fifteen a year would be allowed in.

Generally, it can be said that the standard applied is: fewer, but richer. Those seeking residence in 1971, for example, produced something like £150,000 in tax yield; the newcomers of 1972 yielded £250,000; and in the first nine months of 1973 this doubled to £500,000. This increase was partly accounted for by rising interest rates producing higher incomes. None the less, those who arrived in the three years up to 1974 produced an income of about £1 million. 'The island stands to benefit much more from three immigrants yielding £10,000 apiece than from ten immigrants yielding £3,000 of tax apiece', in the words of the *Pattern of Development*.

Round the inside of the dome in Jersey's Bibliothèque Publique are four names: Shakespeare, Goethe, Dante and the Norman poet Wace. On this doctrine none would have been eligible as settlers in Jersey; nor would Beethoven or Rembrandt. As for Jesus of Nazareth, there might be room at the inn—if reservations are made early enough—but he can scarcely expect to be regarded as 'socially desirable'.

In the past the Jerseyman had tended to regard his low taxes as nothing more than a piece of national good fortune, reflecting no doubt his own financial and governmental acumen. The 'cheap money' period of the late 1950s and early 1960s directed his attention to the fact that it was something on which, in a world of high taxes, he might capitalize. Even before the repeal of the *Code*, Jersey had become a banking centre comparable with Zurich. There were two reasons for this. One was that there were many people working outside the UK whose earnings were still in sterling. If this money was remitted to Britain for investment it would attract tax; by banking through Jersey this was avoided. The other was that many British companies had discovered that by maintaining a registered office in Jersey they, too, could benefit from its low taxes. The doors of advocates' offices were soon bedecked with plates listing dozens of companies, some of them world-famous names, whose registered offices were therein. The suggestion was even made that Jersey registration should be extended to 'flags of convenience' for shipping, but because of a fear that this would sting the British government into action was never pursued.

There was, in any case, a feeling that, to avoid killing the goose that laid golden eggs by forcing Britain's hand, some sort of control of company registrations was necessary. Measures were taken to restrict those which proposed to trade in Britain, but as a blanket prohibition of this kind would obviously cause hardship, since the island only existed by carrying on trade with Britain, the bailiff was given some discretion in permitting company registrations. The partial ban was, however, sufficient to bring into existence a curious trade. Unable to register new companies, there was a brisk sale for old-established Jersey companies, which were free to trade in the UK, particularly those whose articles of association were wide enough to allow them to carry on almost any type of business.

From about 1962, the British merchant banks began moving in. Among the first were the Royal Trust Company of Canada; Kleinwort Benson; and Hill Samuel. In 1965, Rothschilds and Hambros moved in; in 1969, came the first American arrival, First National City, one of the world's major banking houses. By 1972, when the sterling area had shrunk to include only the UK, the Isle of Man, Eire, Gibraltar and the Channel Islands, there were twenty-nine deposit-taking organisations in Jersey. Whole blocks of shops in St Helier were demolished to become their offices. The characteristic landmarks of the town were torn down and sturdy buildings of Jersey granite made way for edifices of concrete, glass and steel, often hideously incongruous in their setting.

At this point the authorities began to take serious account of mounting public unease. Other considerations apart, the conversion of the island into a financial centre was, it was felt, making Jersey unnecessarily and unpleasantly money-conscious. Where once the great matters of bar-debate were cattle or crops, or the latest hotel extension and what it was costing, now it was of investment profits and coups. Banks were making a heavy call on island amenities and services, especially housing and were often successful in persuading the authorities that some new recruit to their staffs should be let in as an 'essential employee'. Besides the growth of banking itself, there was an accompanying increase in other ancillary activities, such as accountancy, law, stockbroking and investment management, most of which, because of lack of locally available skills, generated increased population.

With the failure of two banks—the Guarantee Trust of Jersey Limited and of the Walford Banking Company—and with inquiries pending from some twenty-six banks wanting to open in Jersey, the States decided in 1972 that until the overall value of banking had been assessed no more licences would be granted. After two years of deliberation, policy guidelines were drawn up; emphasis was to be placed on encouraging those activities which produced the most income with the least use of local resources. In the words of *The Pattern of Development*: 'High labour to income ratio activities, such as handling of small trust and small customer current account facilities, should be discouraged, as also should be the cutting of the cake into smaller pieces through the multiplicity of money broking, stockbroking and other financial service activities.' Three or four banks of 'suitable stature' were to be allowed in over a period of about five years; the first to benefit from this concession was the important Algemene Bank of Holland.

To avoid the necessity of importing labour, local training was developed and there are now banking courses at the States College of Further Education. The banks have also been made responsible for providing accommodation for their own staffs brought into the island. This measure has done a little to alleviate the pressure and as the housing permission is granted to the employer, not the occupants, the actual population is kept steady. There have, however, been cases where heavy-handedness has aroused local animosity against the system.

The application of what might seem like policies of restriction have not so far had any appreciable effect on the flow of money, however. By April 1974, the merchant banks operating in Jersey were said to have at their disposal about £900 million in funds and by the end of that year the figure had risen to £1,000 million, much of it lent to London on short call. A significant proportion of these deposits are provided by British residents and banks account for 10 per cent of domestic income.

An indication of local wealth can be gauged from the fact that the Jersey Trustee Savings Bank, which was established with the small saver in mind, has over £70 million in deposits, representing £559 per head of population, compared with £50 per head in UK trustee savings' banks.

Currency

The island introduced its own currency in 1961, though this was not entirely an innovation since an earlier separate coinage had existed for centuries. The *livre tournois*, the traditional basis of the currency from Norman times, had been replaced by pounds, shillings and pence in the 1830s, but the new money was linked with the old by a decree that the halfpenny should equal the old sou and that 520 sous should make up £1. Gradually, as trade with Britain increased and tourists and settlers brought their own money to the island, the British and Jersey currencies reached parity, though consideration was given to introducing decimal currency in the 1870s.

For many years there was no local money, but a shortage of small change during the German Occupation led to the States printing notes in the denominations of 6d, 1s, 3s, 10s and £1, to a total value of £65,000. On the principle that bad money will push out good, these were quickly ousted by the occupation scrip.

The currency introduced in 1961 bears the names and values of British coinage but is not legal tender outside the island, a fact that enables the States to profit from it. It pays its own workers in Jersey notes and encourages all employers to do the same. This obliges the banks to hold considerable sums of island currency and these are obtained by exchanging the British currency with which they are supplied at the States Treasury. In this way, in exchange for a currency without validity outside the island, the treasury gains substantial amounts of one which is; this is then invested in Britain at interest. Thus, the exchange has amounted to an interest-free loan from the banks.

THE COMMON MARKET

In the 1960s Britain's proposed membership of the European Economic Community raised a fundamental constitutional problem for Jersey. The island does not conduct its own foreign policy, but, since 1950, has been automatically excluded from all treaties signed by the British government unless it specifically requested inclusion. In the case of the Treaty of Rome, however, such automatic exclusion was impossible for, under Article 227 (4), European territories of a member-country for whose external affairs that country was responsible would be included in any Community treaty.

Jersey felt that this treaty, perhaps more important than any other in its history, was one whose merits it must decide for itself. Membership of the EEC raised issues fundamentally affecting its life and future. There was, for example, the declared objective of introducing parity of taxation among member countries which would have raised local direct taxes and introduced indirect one entirely new.

Two groups, whose interests were in many ways mutually contradictory, began to make common cause. One was the body of wealthy British immigrants who saw themselves losing the very advantage which had drawn them toward Jersey—its low taxes. The other was a group of conservatively minded Jerseymen who feared the loss of independence. They united to form the Jersey Constitutional Association.

The constitutional question was whether Britain possessed the right to bind the island to a treaty which would affect its internal affairs. A States' Constitutional and Common Market Committee (ConCom for short) was formed and began discussions with the British government.

The British side made clear that for its part there was no intention of allowing negotiations with Brussels to be jeopardised by the Channel Islands. The Jersey leaders were told in secret that, if they did not care for whatever terms Britain's negotiators agreed to, they would be free to break off all links. In other words, accept or get out! Though there were some who felt the gravity of the issue was such as to justify even this course, it was held generally that a step whose long-term effects needed careful assessment was not to be taken lightly.

Britain, however, had responded to the representations made to it to undertake not to commit the island to any treaty without informing it and allowing time for discussion and consent. It then applied for an associate agreement for the island under Article 238 of the Treaty of Rome. This is a clause covering independent third countries. In Brussels, on the other hand, it was ruled that the island would have to come under Article 227 (4). Nevertheless, the agreement to seek island consent had been a species of half-victory which shortly became total. Somewhat to the surprise of many observers, in view of the uncompromising terms of Article 227 (4), the EEC negotiators agreed to treat the islands as a separate, special case.

The nature of the special case then had to be settled. What the island was after was an associate link by which it would be in for trading purposes, but out for all others, such as taxation. The island explained that it had not, like other places, set out to make itself a tax-haven, but had become so through its own thrift and the accident of a long history. To alter this position would be to so endanger its position that it might become a depressed area and in need of aid.

In a word, the island wanted all the benefit of reduced customs tariffs for its goods, but felt unable to accept the responsibilities—an unusually audacious example of a community wanting to have its cake and eat it.

Incredibly, it got what it asked—largely, it is said, because its case was presented at the end of a long round of negotiations when all involved were exhausted. There was one caveat:

henceforward any advantages enjoyed in the islands by UK citizens would apply also to all EEC citizens, and conversely any restrictions on EEC citizens would, in equity, also apply to those from the UK.

Between 1961 and 1973 the wages of States' workers—which are at least an approximate yardstick of other wage levels—rose 170 per cent, while the cost of living increased by about 80 per cent, thus giving a gain in living standards of 90 per cent over the period. Wage earners accounted for 22 per cent of tax paid in 1969.

There has since been a continuing rise in States revenues and in the level of prosperity, with a corresponding improvement in the standard of living. Increasing wealth, the introduction of services of all kinds and the complexification of administration has led to the enlargement of the civil service. It is a matter of some pride that, although taxes represent only 13 per cent of the Gross National Product against Britain's 30 per cent, the States spends on essential services sums comparable on a per capita basis with the UK. These services require operation and there are now some 1,008 civil servants as well as 3,870 public employees at work. The cost to the island has been put at £10,690,000.

To maintain the present level of government spending—and this is bound to rise—the sum taken in income tax alone must increase by at least 3–4 per cent per annum, or by £500,000 in real money, over the coming years. But even these figures presuppose an inflation rate, over which Jersey has no control, of £1·5 million.

Nevertheless, an annual Gross National Product rate of 8 per cent is bettered only by Japan—no small achievement for an island of 72,000 people with no natural resources.

Overseas aid

The island has for some time appreciated the anomaly of its prosperity in a world where there is so much poverty and hardship. To try to offer what assistance it could to territories perhaps comparable with itself, but more needy, the States appointed an Overseas Aid Committee in 1968. Its terms of reference were to see how contributions out of States funds could be applied to the relief of distress in communities overseas. From a contribution of £14,000 in that first year, the figure rose to £100,000 by 1973 and has remained at this level. Among countries now receiving Jersey aid in one form or another are the Seychelles Islands, Swaziland, Mauritius, Zaire, Haiti, India, Kenya, the Gilbert and Ellice Islands, Monserrat, South Korea, Ethiopia and Bangladesh.

Every effort is made to see that maximum benefit is obtained. Jersey teachers, for example, have been seconded to schools in the Seychelles; in exchange, Seychellois teachers are sent to Jersey and have their salaries brought up to local standards by the committee, which is also responsible for their accommodation. Jersey cattle have also been given to the island. In Swaziland a health centre has been opened and was recently extended with Jersey funds. The island has contributed to other educational and health schemes, and to disaster relief; it has completely financed a boys' town in India, assisted underdeveloped agricultures and well-digging projects, and provided funds for such relief organisations as Oxfam and War on Want.

7   INDUSTRY AND EMPLOYMENT

THE GROWTH OF TOURISM

ALTHOUGH tourism had been providing an increasing proportion of the island's income in the inter-war years, it was after 1945 that it began to make its biggest gains. Each year from then on showed a dramatic increase on the previous one and, whenever it seemed that a plateau had been reached, good fortune intervened to give it a new upward impetus. In the early 1950s, for example, there were signs of recession; then in 1956 came the Suez War. Petrol rationing was introduced almost throughout Europe, but the island authorities, believing stocks to be sufficient, decided it was unnecessary. Thousands who had planned a holiday on the continent came instead to Jersey and what had looked like being a year of retrenchment became instead one of the most profitable ever.

Many interacting factors have combined to make the island's originally modest tourist trade into the world's most successful. There was, to begin with, postwar affluence and the increase in paid holidays. Thousands were taking their holidays away from Britain for the first time and Jersey fitted the bill for many of them. It was not too far away. There were no currency, language or even food problems. It was British enough to be reassuring, and different enough to add a spice of adventure, especially when reaching it entailed a plane flight. There was also the undeniable attraction of cheap cigarettes and liquor.

What was more, as a holiday resort, it was itself cheap—at least initially. The economics were to change in Jersey's disfavour, with the introduction of package tours to European resorts, but by that time the island had built up a 'brand image' and loyalty. Thousands of people from all over Britain come to the island year after year and would feel deprived if for any reason they were unable to do so. In a world of inflation Jersey continues to offer good value for the holidaymaker.

While other places may have similar advantages of climate, scenery, sandy beaches and clean sea, few can claim the success of Jersey as a holiday centre. One or two statistics will make this clear: the number of passengers arriving in the island in 1961 was 646,000; it was even then being said that the island had too many visitors and should reduce them by going for quality rather than quantity. None the less, by 1971 the number was up to 870,000 and by 1974 well over the million mark. It has been calculated that taking the year as a whole there are more than ten tourists to every member of the resident population.

The effect on trade gives the measure of tourism's importance to the economy. The island imports £42 million worth of goods a year, but the value of exports is only £19 million. Earnings from tourism more than compensate for this balance of trade deficit, leaving a credit balance of £13·4 million. Total tourist expenditure, excluding fares to the island, at £26 million accounts for 47 per cent of the Gross Domestic Product, that is to say, of the aggregated personal incomes of everybody in the island. Of the money taken by the States Treasury in duties, 50 per cent comes from tourist spending. By 1971, this spending amounted to £30 million, a figure equivalent to 40,000–50,000 residents, but without the cost to society in terms of services, housing, etc. In fact the cost to the resident of the tourism industry is of the order of £1 million a year.

The growing importance of tourism as an economic asset made the local government realise as early as 1948 that everything possible must be done to safeguard it. The island's dependence was such that a 10 per cent drop in visitors would produce a 5 per cent reduction in Gross Domestic Product, reflected immediately in a rise in unemployment. What the authorities were particularly concerned about was the quality of accommodation and facilities offered to holidaymakers.

Tourist accommodation

The States Committee of Tourism decided, therefore, to introduce a system of compulsory registration of all hotels and guest houses catering for more than five people and to grade each establishment according to size of rooms, facilities, night services, staff efficiency, cuisine, quality of furnishings, situation and appearance, number of rooms with baths, showers, telephones, etc. Teams from the École Hotelière of Paris were brought to the island to do the initial grading and four registers were established. The first was for top-category hotels, which are graded by suns, the maximum number awarded to any hotel being four; the second was for smaller hotels, graded in up to four diamonds; the third was for guest houses, which are graded A, B and C, and the fourth for holiday camps. Both registration and grading have to appear on the entrance of the establishment and must be printed on all its stationery and letterheads.

The system goes into very great detail. Hotels in the first and second registers, for instance, are required to have bedrooms not smaller than 600cu ft, of which 70sq ft must be room space, while there must be at least 10sq ft of window area. Periodically, the standards are raised and to retain its grading within a particular register an establishment must improve its facilities. The system works well and the Tourism Department's inspectors are no longer looked upon as ogres, though they can be called upon to investigate a complaint and can order the summary closure of an establishment. 'Customer appreciation' is shown by the fact that in 1970, 544,000 out of 819,000 visitors stayed in registered accommodation.

Investment in tourist accommodation has increased steadily and at one time eagerness to get into it was such that there was concern about the spiralling prices of hotels in the island. Over the years many new hotels have been built and new extensions added; modest guest houses in the backstreets of St Helier or in outlying country districts burgeoned into large hotels with all modern amenities down to their own private swimming-pools. By 1970 there was a total of 26,000 beds available. There has been a slight decrease since, although the number of visitors has actually risen; this is mainly accounted for by a longer season and a more economic usage of facilities.

The Jersey Hotel and Guest House Association, which represents the interests of the hotel industry, has some 600 members and so includes almost every establishment on the island. Various sub-committees are responsible for such matters as law, staff employment and advertising, and among its activities is the production of the holiday brochure *Invitation to Jersey* of which some 200,000 copies are distributed through the Tourism Department annually. Besides providing a permanent office in St Helier with secretarial services, a staff employment bureau and a regular newsletter, the association also organises a gastronomic festival, a *salon culinaire* and a very popular waiters' and waitresses' race.

All establishments are required to declare a tariff for the coming season, but to take account of inflation a second, higher one, can be declared; this is a fixed-percentage increase on the basic price and comes into effect, if necessary, from mid-summer.

In return for the association's co-operation in maintaining the quality and price stability of accommodation, the Tourism

Department gives a great deal of active help to the industry. It spends large sums in advertising and publicity; for the 1974 season the total appropriation was £369,000. This included advertising space in magazines, in national and provincial newspapers, and on television, in Britain, Holland, France and Belgium. Big publicity campaigns have also been mounted in the United States in recent years.

This direction of effort towards the continent and North America is indicative of a widening in the market for holidays in Jersey. The total number of visitors from places other than the UK, which stood at 4,698 in 1950, had risen to 170,864 by 1973. France, not unexpectedly in view of its proximity, provided the greatest number, some 141,427, but visitors from the United States, 150 in 1950, were up to 1,658 by 1973. Visitors from Britain still predominate, however, and account for something like 90 per cent of tourist expenditure.

Entertainment complex and conference centre

In 1958 the States had acquired Fort Regent, a big area of barrack blocks, parade grounds and military stores on the rocky promontory overlooking St Helier. After turning down an offer from the Hilton group to build a hotel and casino there, it was decided that the site should be used to provide three amenities which the island lacked: a conference hall large enough to accommodate international-size conventions; an indoor swimming-pool, and an entertainment complex for holidaymakers when the weather was bad. It would house an International-size swimming-pool, sports arena, cafés, children's playgrounds, walks, solarium, squash courts and piazzas. A large rotunda capable of seating 2,000 delegates would be used for conferences. The development would take ten years to complete and cost an estimated £2·5 million.

To pay for this States enterprise, a lottery was introduced in 1966, with prizes ranging from £5 up to the thousands, and

Plate 11 St Martin's church: (*left*) a detail from the exterior of the church; (*below*) the church itself. Notwithstanding the Victorian appearance of the steeple, this is the oldest church on the island, regarded as ancient even in the reign of William I.

Plate 12 (left) The Fishermen's chapel, St Brelade, once a private chantry. Its walls are decorated with murals depicting the Annunciation, the Massacre of the Innocents, the Entry into Jerusalem, the Scourging, the Crucifixion, the Resurrection and the Last Judgment.

Plate 12 (right) The grave of Lily Langtry, née Le Breton, the Edwardian actress and beauty, at St Saviour's Church.

the profits were devoted to the execution of the scheme. The swimming-pool was opened, gardens and children's play-grounds were laid out and a cable-car system installed to carry visitors up the 85ft from St Helier to the fort. It is a guide to the success of the whole enterprise that by 1974 this had carried a million passengers.

The plans for the rotunda conference centre were ambitious: a great shallow-dome roof was built over the old parade ground; with a diameter of 170ft, it is the second largest roof span in Europe. While work was proceeding it was discovered that there were difficulties in transporting delegates to and from the rotunda when it was in use as a conference centre. The cable-car system was obviously not designed to carry large numbers in a short time and the intention had been that coaches would be used, following the original roads leading up to the fort. But these were narrow and winding, with hairpin bends, and there was little space for manoeuvre at the top. It was estimated that it would have taken something like six hours to move 2,000 people from the rotunda. There was talk of the conference centre as a £1·2 million 'white elephant', and this seemed justified when a St Helier hotel announced its intention of building a conference hall of its own, which would have the advantage of accommodation and catering being pro-vided on the spot.

The overall cost of the whole Fort Regent project had risen from the original estimate to £5·5 million and there was an angry debate in the States, with one senator referring to the entire enterprise as 'the worst example of incompetence' he had known in twenty-four years in the House. The President of the Fort Regent Committee resigned and, when a new one was appointed, the States decided that they wanted a closer control of the scheme and stipulated that henceforward money needed would have to be requested annually.

From this point work proceeded smoothly and one possible

solution to the problem of transport which is still under consideration is the installation of escalators in three flights at a cost of some £265,000.

Trends in tourism

Jersey was never, despite constant wooing, deeply involved in the package-holiday business, with its accompanying movement of travel agents into the hotel industry. On the contrary, the island's hoteliers themselves formed into groups and became travel agents, selling tours to their own establishments. Not only did they operate on a sounder basis by doing so, but it was felt they could offer a more dedicated and professional expertise in the hotel trade than any travel agent was likely to do.

One change in the island's tourist pattern was brought about by the introduction of a car-ferry service. Many more visitors were arriving without booking accommodation in advance, and their case could only be met by a drastic increase in the number of campsites.

The island hopes to make fuller use of its tourist establishments in the 'shoulder months' on either side of the high season, by expanding its conference business and by publicising the pleasures of Jersey during off-peak periods. To encourage this, a spring festival, including a variety of events, has been inaugurated. It is estimated that filling the hotels at these off-season times would bring in at least another £1 million, but it would also create a staffing problem. Most of those working in tourist establishments are recruited from Spain and Portugal—formerly they came from Italy as well—and return home during the winter months when the hotels and guest houses close. An indefinite extension of the tourist season would mean that the itinerant labour would become permanently residential, putting pressure on the existing pool of housing and other services.

Labour is, however, becoming increasingly difficult to find.

INDUSTRY AND EMPLOYMENT

As one by one the countries of Southern Europe improve their living standards, fewer and fewer of their workpeople are prepared to make the journey to Jersey for employment for only part of the year. Furthermore, the island's reputation as an employer of labour has by no means always been a good one; it is largely due to the low wages paid to these workers that the costs of holidays in Jersey have been kept down. The accommodation provided for hotel staff is often poor and any attempt to improve it, such as by providing staff hostels, is balked by the hoteliers with the argument that it would raise prices and affect the island's competitive position. In 1974 *The Guardian* described living conditions for visiting labour in Jersey as 'varying from the primitive to the slumlike', an assessment with which it is difficult to disagree. Complaints made by the various national consuls on the island have threatened to explode into international incidents, but there has been no real effort to improve the situation.

The labour problem seems to be only one of the factors now placing a limitation of growth in the tourist trade. Since the massive expansion of the 1950s and early 1960s, there is now a levelling out. Between 1961 and 1971, receipts from the tourist industry went up by only 8·5 per cent—the lowest increase of all the main sources of public revenue. The economists, however, remain optimistic; according to their forecasts, Jersey ought to continue to attract some 650,000 visitors a year from the UK and another 100,000 from Western Europe.

AGRICULTURE

In the late 1950s a special committee of the Jersey States was assigned the sensitive task of defining the relationship between the various major contributors to the common wealth and to the form of its development. This, of course, included agriculture, which had become a very diversified industry, despite

III

the size of the island. Although potatoes held the lion's share in terms of land usage, there were in addition tomatoes, flowers, broccoli, milk, meat, poultry and eggs, besides some other vegetables grown mainly for home consumption. While it had been realised for some time that agriculture was failing to keep abreast of other sources in terms of income produced, the committee's report showed that it was actually declining and, indeed, has continued to do so.

The island's total land area is 64,612 vergées—the vergée is a local land measure equal to four-ninths of an acre. In 1951, some 57,250 vergées were given over to agriculture; by 1961, this had fallen to 40,000 vergées and by 1973, to 39,302. Many of the island's bigger farmhouses had been sold off to wealthy immigrants and the number of farmers had fallen from 1,666 in 1961 to 1,118 in 1971. What was more, with the exception of milk production, output was falling everywhere. Potato production, for instance, had declined from 56,800 tons to 47,150 over roughly the same period. By 1973, it was down to 44,000 tons and, in 1974, to 27,000. This was admittedly an exceptional year because of a protracted drought, but farmers, now facing competition in the British market from other parts of Europe, are asking whether their potato exports will ever reach 40,000 tons again.

Even sadder, if only for reasons of sentiment, is the fate of the Jersey cattle export industry. Not only has the Jersey cow gained a world-wide reputation, but it made an enormous contribution to the survival of the islanders during the war. The animal which required no special feedstuff even in the depth of winter and continued to give milk of tremendous nutritional value helped to make good desperate shortages of almost every other essential.

The immediate post-war years had brought an immediate boom as depleted herds throughout the world were replenished so that over an eight-year period annual exports averaged something like 2,000 a year. Buyers came not only from Britain, but from the USA, South Africa, Turkey and even the USSR. A mere handful now leaves the island, at most worth about £100,000 a year to the island and by some estimated at only £30,000.

The coarsening which afflicts the breed when divorced from its island pastures, since it does not affect milk yield, has been found tolerable, so that the main buyers are now breeders anxious to show. At the same time, the differences in the subsidies paid by governments for premium quality milk over ordinary qualities is not sufficient to justify the added expense.

The overall picture is thus one in which between 1961 and 1971, in real money values, there was no increase in tax payments by people employed in agriculture. The whole situation is somewhat callously summed up in a sentence in *The Pattern of Development*: 'It is not expected that agriculture will make any real contribution to income growth in the future.'

It is the landscape of shady meadows with their browsing cattle, of fields and those steeply rising hillsides the islanders call *côtils*, bearing their ripening crops, which are the 'rural amenity' attracting alike holidaymaker and wealthy settler. For this reason the island simply cannot afford to put its agricultural life in jeopardy. And in terms of community value it provided some 10 per cent of the Gross Domestic Product in 1968, so that diminution would mean the loss of many jobs to the island. What is more, agricultural goods shipped out represent an important 'visible' export—indeed the island's principal one. Of the £19 million worth of goods exported in 1969, 40 per cent came from this source. But how is agriculture to be preserved in such a way as will keep the proud and independent Jersey farmer in business as other than a state-subsidised 'tourist attraction'?

Intensification and consolidation

The answers found elsewhere have been intensification and the consolidation of farms into fewer but larger and more economic holdings. Of these the first offers only limited scope for exploitation. Local agriculture has always been, by the nature of the place, intensive and has become progressively more so. The island farmer, with his small holding—the average is 34 vergées (15 acres)—long ago learnt that he must use to the full his advantages of climate and a soil of such fertility that in some cases potatoes have been grown on the same land for fifty consecutive seasons, to produce early yielding, high-return crops. At the same time ruthless attempts to intensify might be as destructive of amenities as a greater decline in agriculture as a whole. The result could well be, as in the north of Guernsey, a landscape turned into an unappealing vista of glasshouses.

In the main, then, the resolution of the farmer's troubles must lie in consolidation, counterbalanced, unless he wants to see an agonising reduction in numbers, by co-operation. In the former there have been great strides. Holdings of 1–50 vergées, which in 1967 represented 81·3 per cent of the total land in use, had shrunk to 72·4 per cent by 1973. At the same time holdings of 50–100 vergées, only 18·9 per cent in 1967, were up to 27·6 per cent by 1973. By the same token, while the number of herds of cattle dropped from 473 in 1969 to 344 in 1973, the average number of cows per herd went up from 11 to 13·8.

Taken over a longer period the figures are still more revealing. In 1953 there were 1,808 holdings of 1–50 vergées and only 198 above this size. By 1973, the 1–50 vergées holdings had tumbled to 747 and the larger had risen to 284. The total number of holdings had dropped from 2,006 to 1,031, in other words a fall of nearly 100 per cent, though the reduction in land usage was only about 11 per cent.

However, linked to the problem of consolidation is that of land tenure. In a place with such a density of population, land prices will obviously be high and price will reflect itself in rentals charged. This is a particularly serious problem for Jersey where only 37·5 per cent of land is owned by farmers while 62·5 is rented. To exacerbate the position, development land can command a price as much as seven times as high as that for agricultural land. States policy and legislation have been directed therefore to avoiding the loss of agricultural land, while ensuring reasonable safeguards for the owner who wanted to sell, and to giving the farmer security of tenure. This last is particularly important if he is to be encouraged to increase the size and efficiency of his operation. If rented land which he had improved or developed was suddenly taken from him, his effort and investment would obviously be wasted.

Co-operation
The progress of co-operation faces an obstacle of a different kind. This is the notoriously stubborn individualism of the Jersey farmer. A producer-owned milk marketing board was set up in 1953 by an almost unanimous vote, largely because producers had fresh in their memories the experience of gross exploitation by the dairymen in the inter-war period. On the other hand, attempts to form a potato marketing board, repeatedly made over a period of something like a decade, were constantly balked, despite government approval and the admirable case made out for it by its sponsors. One of the reasons for this opposition was the failure of the Tomato Panel, which existed between 1946 and 1949, to respond to a buyer's market situation in that last year. Because of this growers felt themselves denied large profits.

This is not to say the local farmer lives in a state of cold isolation from his neighbours. The Royal Jersey Agricultural and Horticultural Society has now been representing the interest of farmers since 1833 and at present has some 477 members in its agricultural department alone. In particular, it has done much to further the career of the Jersey cow and at its own ground at Springfield, St Helier, holds spring, summer and autumn shows which attract buyers from all parts of the world. Its horticultural interests are advanced by shows held in early summer, summer and autumn, all of which draw large numbers of entries of high standard. In recent years much of its activity has been assumed by the Jersey Farmers' Union, formed in 1919, which functions in much the same way as the National Farmers' Union in Britain, acting in liaison with the government, for example. It is also responsible for the distribution of seasonal workers from abroad, and at present represents 345 local farmers. The interests of flower growers are represented by another organisation, the Jersey Bulb and Flower Growers' Association, though this may shortly merge with the JFU.

It is also fair to say that former attitudes are changing as a new and more pragmatic generation of farmers and growers replaces the old. Perhaps, too, before the chilling facts of decline, the need for co-operation is being appreciated more keenly than heretofore. Local economists, having weighed the situation up, have declared that it is still regarded as feasible for the island to support a farming community high in proportion to the population overall. In general, agriculture is seen less as under the threat of total or near extinction than as faced by a number of problems, some difficult, yet all capable of solution.

States assistance

Possibly the most hopeful sign is that, where a decade or so ago there was a feeling among the agricultural community that they had been overlooked by the States, today this has ceased to be true. Compared with the farmers of Europe, including

Britain, who receive government aid in the form of subsidies or interventions of between 10 and 20 per cent of the value of their output, those in Jersey still fare less well, but where a few years ago the States contributed only about 1 per cent, since 1973 this has risen to 5 per cent.

In consequence, public spending must be as cautious in agriculture as it is everywhere else. Each problem needs careful analysis and evaluation and every pound directed towards the most efficient solution of it. Fortunately, the small size of the island and the smallness in proportion of the farming community makes this possible. Thanks to the enlightened policy of the Committee of Agriculture and its executive arm, the States Department of Agriculture, not only is assistance given in very many ways, but a whole comprehensive range of services is offered in addition.

The Agricultural Loans and Guarantee Scheme offers subsidised loans to both tenant and owner farmers, and to those just coming into agriculture, for various building and improvement purposes, or for land-purchase. The loans cover up to two-thirds of the value and are repayable over a maximum of forty years at an interest rate well below the market one. Hundreds of thousands of pounds have already been lent in this way. There has been less enthusiasm for the Guarantee Scheme by which the committee acts as bank guarantor on behalf of a farmer for loans for improvement, developments and working capital. This is probably because of high interest rates.

The greatest beneficiaries from States' support are undoubtedly the milk producers. Milk presents a special case in that this is one of the few commodities which farmers actually sell on the home market. This situation will ultimately change as, under the terms of its associate membership of the European Economic Community, the island can no longer prevent the entry of milk from Europe. It is likely to be some time before changes are implemented and, in the meantime, it is essential to ensure that there is sufficient milk for local needs, remembering especially the heavy demands of tourism in the summer.

As a matter of both cost and principle the States does not subsidise the consumer price of milk. Thus, there comes about the paradox in which those living in a place world-famous for milk-cattle pay considerably more than those elsewhere. It is felt, however, that charging the full economic price helps to control consumption. To avoid hardship, old people, expectant mothers and children receive cheap milk.

The method chosen to encourage the producer in his seven-day-a-week job has been to pay a bonus at a fixed rate per gallon for all registered cattle which produce more than a qualifying minimum quantity in a specified lactation. The scheme appears to work well and some £180,000 was set aside for it in the 1974 States' estimates, representing the biggest single item in the Committee of Agriculture's budget.

Marketing

Second to this in cost come the Export Incentive Bonuses, costing something like £160,000 a year. They represent a step in a long-term campaign by the committee to rationalise marketing. It can record some success, for if the notion of a single, central marketing organisation did not attract the local grower, the old system of sending to market through merchants or even individually has given place to co-operatives. There are some five of these in existence to handle edible crops and they are jointly responsible for something like 99·9 per cent of the potato crop. Similar developments have taken place in the island's other two main crops, tomatoes and broccoli, about 85 per cent of which are now exported through the same co-operative. As a means of advancing co-operative activity the Department of Agriculture pays out a bonus of about £2 a ton on all produce so exported.

In the hope of further rationalising the situation and to

produce a degree of co-operation between the co-operatives themselves, a marketing federation has now been formed to which all these groups are affiliated. There have now been moves to improve the organisation of flower marketing in similar ways. The committee have offered financial assistance in promoting sales to the Continent to all flower-marketing bodies prepared to form co-operatives and to work closely together; three of the flower exporters have now formed a Flower Section of the federation.

A further £60,000 is paid out in various direct subsidies for crop protection and fertilisers. These are aimed at keeping the most common pests under control and at ensuring that the soil is maintained in an adequately fertile condition. All fertilisers and pesticides have to be imported and this is reflected in their price to the island grower.

Services

Quite separate from this sort of financial aid is the whole spectrum of services offered by the Department of Agriculture. A free farm management and advisory service includes soil analysis, information on various aspects of agriculture and husbandry, a weather service, pest and disease diagnosis, crop trials and freely available management advice. In addition, the States veterinary officers offer assistance on all matters of animal health and on their importation and exportation. There is a herd-recording scheme which provides breeders with month-by-month details of the production of each of his animals. A statistical summary published annually affords a basis for assessing trends in the industry. A farm secretarial service is available on a contract basis and will, if asked, establish a simple accountancy scheme which has been worked out for farmers. A produce inspectorate checks that all exports satisfy the statutory requirements in force for them. To help keep the name of Jersey produce before the buying public a specialist advertising agency in Britain is employed and this also provides a market research service. In the 1974 estimates an appropriation of £75,000 was set aside for publicity.

States Experimental Farm

In 1938, a Jersey boy who had emigrated to South Africa and there made his fortune, died. To his homeland, in memory of his son Howard, killed in World War I, he left a number of magnificent bequests, including an area of land to the east of St Helier now laid out as a beautiful park. Howard Hall was presented to Victoria College, the local public school, as well as scholarships to the school and to the university for twenty-five local boys. The island also received a new lifeboat and a farm at Trinity. Attached to this last gift was the request that it should be used for the benefit of the agricultural community as a whole.

It became the States' Experimental Farm, which has done much useful work. Its 14 acres of croppable land and 20,000sq ft of heated glass are used as a demonstration farm where growers can see established and potential crops being grown under local conditions by various techniques. This last aspect of its work has particular relevance in view of the widely felt need for growers to seek other ways of increasing the range of their produce. The farm is administered by the Committee of Agriculture, through a Farm Advisory Panel and a farm manager. It represents therefore yet another service available to the farmer and to extend its activities an extra 11 acres of croppable land is now rented.

Land tenure and labour

Much thought is now being given to the question of reforming the land tenure laws in such a way as to ensure the farmer's security and justify his expenditure of capital and other resources, while not placing a punitive restriction upon the owner's right to sell.

INDUSTRY AND EMPLOYMENT

As far as skilled labour is concerned, there has been a marked shift from the land because of poor wages and lack of status. Measures taken to reverse this trend include the foundation of an agricultural and horticultural education centre at the Howard Davis Farm. This operates on a part-time basis for students already working in these industries and encourages suitable ones to go on to further courses at farm institutes in Britain. Development of skill will, it is hoped, increase both the pay and prestige attaching to work on the land, hitherto regarded as the last resort of the least bright members of the community.

Of unskilled labour, on the other hand, the agricultural community has an intermittent need and local people being unwilling to accept employment on this sporadic basis, it has had to be imported, mainly from northern France. As with tourism, the island has gained a bad reputation for its treatment of labour and the French consul warned that if improvements were not made his government might ban the recruitment of workers. In any event, rising standards of living in France itself and the availability of more permanent employment has made recruiting difficult. Skilled labourers from Brittany, who were in some ways the best to be found and tended to live semi-permanently in the island, have been largely replaced by Portuguese workers.

The Department of Agriculture, which has long been urging improvements in living conditions, anticipates a continuing need for such imported labour during the seasonal peaks, but confidently expects better techniques to reduce and perhaps finally abolish this need.

FISH PRODUCTION

Astonishing as it would have seemed only a decade ago, there are signs of a revival in fish production—the term is used advisedly, for the activities now being carried on are for the most part something quite different from the traditional hunting of the seas and more akin to its cultivation.

To a large extent this has concentrated itself on shellfish. In 1961, an attempt to revive the Jersey oyster industry was made when some 12,000 Bretons were laid in St Catherine's Bay. Only 3,000 proved marketable, however, and another laying of 100,000 was no more fortunate, as the entire crop was killed. Not deterred by these setbacks, a firm calling itself La Rocque Fisheries Ltd laid some 25,000 seed oysters in Grouville Bay in March 1974 and the seeds of 100,000 Pacific oysters were put down in St Clement's Bay. A first harvest of Jersey mussels, seeded earlier and gathered in November 1973, was found to be of excellent quality. Recently, too, a fleet of modern vessels began fishing for lobster not only in Channel Island waters, but as far north as the Hebrides, often in appalling weather.

The States has been taking a fresh look at the possibilities of establishing a new industry for the island. Under the auspices of the Harbours and Airport Committee research is being conducted into the island's fishery resources. Experimental scallop and seed mussel beds have been laid between Jersey and Sark and consideration is being given to feasibilities of 'fish farming' or to applying to local waters other experiments now being conducted in the UK, such as shellfish cultivation.

The gathering of ormers has always been controlled by law and those who took them when they were below a certain size were liable to prosecution. Since marine biologists have declared that the ormer is becoming rarer, many people are wondering whether the present laws are adequate. There is deep concern about the depredations of skin-divers on the beds and one proposal is to introduce a total ban on fishing ormers for several years to give a chance for breeding. Tests in Scotland have shown that the ormer can be bred in captivity and it is suggested that this might be a more reliable way of re-stocking.

Fishing limits

Because of the smallness of the fishing industry, Jersey had never troubled to adjust its territorial limits. Its waters still extend only 3 miles from the foreshore and in some places are actually less because of proximity to the French coast, where broader limits are claimed. Local fishermen have long wanted an extension at least to 6 miles, but to make a change at this late stage may be difficult. In any case, it is hard to see how a wider limit can be maintained without something in the nature of a fishery protection force.

INDUSTRIAL DEVELOPMENT

There has been some industry in the island since long before the war—the production of the local newspaper and the processing of milk and milk products by the Milk Marketing Board could be included in this category, while the building industry, which in Jersey accounts for 9 per cent of domestic income, is a further example.

The encouragement of a small light industry sector in the economy has for some time been seen as a means not only of diversification but also of giving better job opportunities to school-leavers. Plainly, the only firms likely to be attracted would be those for whom the advantageous tax position would outweigh costs arising from the need to import raw materials and export finished products. All the same, marked success has been achieved and about sixteen companies are now operating in Jersey making goods as varied as knitwear, tape-recorders, shock-absorbers, bedspreads and electronic equipment, apart from local pottery.

Industry now accounts for about 5 per cent of Gross Domestic

Product and about 1,000 people are employed in it. Plans are under consideration for increasing the size of the small trading estate at Rue des Pres on the eastern side of the island or establishing others, and it is anticipated that employment may grow by another 500 in the next decade.

Plate 13 Jersey Zoo, whose particular importance is being the home of the Jersey Wildlife Preservation Trust, is a popular tourist attraction: (*above*) gorillas are one of the species for which the zoo is famous. This is Mamfe, one of four Lowland gorillas born there on 11 September 1973; (*below*) Here Gerald Durrell, the Zoological Director, examines a rare seriema.

Plate 14 Flower cultivation in Jersey: (*left*) gathering the flowers – large scale cultivation takes place on the warm eastern side of the island.

Plate 14 Flower cultivation in Jersey: (*right*) a decorated pony-cart taking part in the Jersey Battle of Flowers, one of the premier events of the summer season. Besides such more modest exhibits the parade includes enormous floats as much as 40ft long, all, like this, covered in flowers.

8 LIFELINES AND SERVICES

THE sea, on which so much of the island's prosperity was based, at one time provided a not unwelcome gulf between it and Britain. The sea-crossing was at best uncomfortable and in winter often prolonged and dangerous; it sometimes took several weeks. By the beginning of the nineteenth century, there were still no proper harbour facilities, only a 200ft breakwater giving shelter to the coves called the English and French Harbours. The Duke of Gloucester, arriving in the island in 1817, had to make an undignified all-fours scramble ashore across the rocks. Later, Prince Albert, reaching the jetty when the tide was low, asked why Jersey's harbour had been built on dry land. Perhaps stung by this comment, the States decided to build a cargo quay and then an esplanade over the dunes south of St Helier to provide an approach from the landward side. In 1837, James Walker was commissioned to plan an entirely new harbour consisting of what came to be called the Victoria and Albert Piers, built from local granite. A more ambitious plan to incorporate Elizabeth Castle into a great outer breakwater was later abandoned, with heavy financial loss, and the authorities resigned themselves to constant dredging to prevent the harbour being silted up by mud dragged in by the huge tides.

By the middle of Victoria's reign steam-packets were plying from England's south coast harbours, drastically reducing the

H

time it took to reach the island, and in 1870 the lighthouse at La Corbière, one of Jersey's best-known landmarks, was built as an aid to safe passage in the treacherous seas.

Harbours continued to serve as the most important gateway to the island until after World War II—and, if one discounts passenger traffic, they still do. Imports represent 70 per cent of the Gross Domestic Product and most of these come by sea; agriculture and horticulture depend for 80 per cent of their income on exports, which, except for flowers, are predominantly seaborne. The fact that between 1938 and 1970 imports rose from 181,721 to 418,432 gross tons, shows the continuing and increasing importance of the harbours. However, the wide variation between the levels of imports, about £42 million, and exports, some £19 million, means that the returning vessels are often not fully laden; even excluding this from the reckoning, the total year-round trade is insufficient for frequent low-cost services, though some improvement could be brought about if the agricultural community could be persuaded to consolidate its marketing arrangements more completely.

Among local shipping companies, Commodore Shipping Services operate cargo- and passenger-carrying hydrofoils between Guernsey and Jersey, and also connect both islands with Sark, Alderney and St Malo.

The principal passenger services are run by British Rail's 'Sealink' mail boats; two modern, stabilised vessels, the *Caesarea* and *Sarnia*, operate out of Weymouth, with interconnecting rail services within the UK for the day or night crossings. There is also a 'Sealink' drive-on drive-off car ferry, which carries ninety vehicles, between Weymouth, Guernsey and Jersey. Reservations are needed for all journeys between April and October and in some cases at Easter and Christmas; these guarantee each passenger a place in the ship, and early booking is essential. Sleeping berths and a small number of cabins are available.

AIRWAYS

The arrival of a seaplane from St Malo in 1912 heralded a new age of transport for the island. By 1925 a flying-boat service provided a regular link and, from 1933, a local company, Jersey Airways, instituted a daily service. At that time aircraft landed on the beach at St Aubin. In 1937 an airport was built at St Peter in the west of the island and the following year it handled 17,500 passengers. Compared with the easy-going tempo with which the harbours were developed, the airport has grown at a fast and consistent pace. Between 1947 and 1970, 17 million passengers have used its vastly extended and modernised facilities; it now claims to be the third busiest airport in the British Isles and 1·5 million passenger movements a year are forecast by 1980.

The use of larger and larger aircraft has called for a number of costly runway extensions, and in 1973 the island was again under criticism from the British Association of Airline Pilots on account of the shortness of runways which it denounced as unsafe. Impeding further extensions, desirable as they may be, is the shortage and high price of land. In Guernsey, where similar difficulties have arisen, thought has been given to abandoning the present airport and building a new 'offshore' one with a 7,000-yard jet runway projecting into the sea; Jersey may have to adopt similar expedients. This is a case for closer co-operation between the two islands and the conclusion may be that there is no need for each island to provide such facilities; one airport with interconnecting ferries might well be the answer.

In any event, airports are likely to remain a heavy, if necessary burden and represent one of those costs which cannot be scaled down to the size of the community. Though Jersey airport is run at a loss which has to be met by the island taxpayer, who is also called on to foot the bill for any extensions, there is already criticism from airline-operating companies that the island's airport dues are the highest in the British Isles. Traffic originating in Jersey accounts for less than 20 per cent of the total carried and while there are nearly a dozen companies operating out of Jersey their services become exiguous in winter when the only traffic is local. Many islanders feel, therefore, that they are supporting the airport for the use of others and it has been suggested that a tourist tax should be introduced to alter this.

The most important of the airline operating companies is British Airways, which carries about 45 per cent of all traffic and, by offering the best year-round service, something like 60 per cent in winter. Others include British Island Airways, British Caledonian, Aer Lingus, British Midland Airways, Dan-Air Skyways, the French independent airline Rousseau Aviation, Intra Airways, J.F. Airlines, Brymon Aviation, and Air Anglia. In 1969 Aurigny Air Services, a subsidiary of a British charter firm, inaugurated a walk-on walk-off bus-stop ferry service, and has carried about a million passengers on its Britten-Norman 'Islander' and larger 'Trislander' aircraft between Jersey, Guernsey and the other islands.

The States Harbours and Airport Committee is responsible not only for the operation of the island's harbours and airport, but for the installation, maintenance and operating of equipment in the busy Channel Islands' Air Traffic Control Zone, in collaboration with Guernsey. The Committee runs a local meteorological office, whose services are used also by yachtsmen, shipping and farmers.

ROADS

At the beginning of the nineteenth century, Jersey's roads were regarded as among the worst in the British Isles. General George Don, appointed lieutenant-governor during the Napoleonic Wars, decided that they were in such a state as to impede the fast movement of his forces should the island be invaded, but his efforts to improve them were not unopposed. When workmen started work on the road which was to run from St Helier to Grouville in the east an irate farmer threatened to shoot the first man who turned a sod. Don himself went to the spot and in full regimentals took a spade and commenced digging. The farmer did not shoot. The general succeeded in building 18 miles of military roads, plus interconnexions; there are now about 150 miles of road in the island and 200 miles of secondary roads. The building of roads is the responsibility of the States Public Works Committee, which also undertakes the maintenance of main roads; the cost of maintaining the minor roads is shared between the island and the parish.

RAILWAYS

In 1870, the Jersey Western Railway was opened from St Helier to St Aubin and was later extended further west to La Corbière. In 1872, a second company, the Eastern Railway, was running services eastward, to Gorey. They continued in operation for a little over fifty years. In 1923, however, the Western Railways was bought out by the Devon Motor Transport Company, which also owned buses and launched the present Jersey Motor Transport Company. In 1929, the Eastern Railway succumbed to the competition of the Safety Coach Service, operating in the east, and it was obvious that buses were a more convenient form of transport since they were able to reach outlying areas not accessible by rail. Trains finally came to an end in 1936, though some small-gauge railways were built by the Germans during the war, following the course of the old tracks. As these were used exclusively by the Wehrmacht, however, it could be said that before the war the island had become totally dependent on bus services.

PUBLIC TRANSPORT

Since the war, the Jersey Motor Transport Company has run all the bus services on the island. It has had to compete with an increasing car ownership and needs to make maximum profits during the summer to tide it over the winter months. The company believes it could better serve the public if it also had something nearer a total monopoly in the tourist coach services, which are at present operated by a number of different firms, mainly on a 'summer only' basis. There has been no real move so far to bring this situation about, though there are occasional demands for nationalisation of all public transport. But it is doubtful, even with a total States' monopoly, whether transport services could ever be made economic, unless private motoring is also curbed. For the first time, this possibility is now receiving serious consideration.

MOTOR TRAFFIC

The whole question of motor traffic is under constant review by the Motor Traffic Office, a department of the Island Defence Committee, which is also responsible for licensing and testing vehicles and the examination of learner-drivers. While millions of pounds have been spent on traffic-flow systems and multi-storey car parks, little has been done to improve public transport or to encourage its use. With the risk of the roads clogging up entirely—there are thirty vehicles to every mile of road—it has even been suggested by the *Evening Post* that substantial tax allowances should be made to people who voluntarily give up private motoring.

Visiting motorists should acquaint themselves with the Jersey Highway Code as traffic laws must be strictly enforced in these overcrowded conditions. Caravans are banned altogether.

Although postal services began in Britain in 1660, it was not for over a century that a mail service with Jersey was inaugurated. Until that time letters sent from the island had to be entrusted to travellers or to the captains of packets. In 1784, post offices were established in Jersey and Guernsey by Act of Parliament, and the first postmaster was appointed in the person of Charles William Le Geyt, who continued to hold the office until 1815, when at the age of eighty-two he retired in favour of his son. There were, at first, no deliveries; letters were simply collected from the postmaster's home, but in 1798 he engaged an elderly woman to deliver in the town. Country deliveries did not begin until 1827. In 1852, the novelist Anthony Trollope, who worked as a post office surveyor, was sent to the island. He suggested the setting up of roadside mailboxes and one was installed in St Helier—the first of its kind in the British Isles.

Postal services in the island were operated by the GPO until 1969 when the Post Office Corporation came into existence. Jersey did not want to be included in this arrangement, with the result that the Insular Postal Administration was formed and, on 1 October 1969, Jersey Post Office took over from the GPO. This enterprise has proved highly successful and by 1973 had made £1 million profit, of which £750,000 was paid into the general revenues of the States. The JPO, under a director of postal administration, has its headquarters in a converted tobacco factory in St Helier; it has also extensively renovated and modernised the main post office in Broad Street.

One reason for its success has been the worldwide popularity among philatelists of the beautifully designed and produced Jersey stamps. Most of these have been printed by the Swiss firm of Courvoisier, though a few have come from the presses of Harrison of Britain. Besides definitives it is usual practice to bring out four commemorative issues a year and these are in particularly high demand among collectors. One of them, a reproduction of a painting by the eighteenth-century island artist, Peter Monamy, of the English fleet in the Channel was placed third among the world's seventy best stamps. To keep pace with demand there is an island philatelic service run by the States and sales from it have already grossed considerable sums.

TELEPHONES

Telephones first came to the island in 1898 when the old National Telephone Company opened an exchange in Minden Place. When the GPO took over its operation, there was a public outcry as it was believed the excellent service would decline. In 1923, the States were given a licence to run their own telephone service, with the GPO retaining the inter-island links until they were taken over by Jersey in 1953.

When Jersey and Guernsey took over the running of their own postal services in 1969, they jointly bought a half share in the trunk cables connecting the islands with Britain—at a cost to Jersey of £1·8 million. A tripartite agreement was drawn up and from 1 January 1973 the two islands and the Post Office Corporation became responsible for trunk communication. Two cables now connect Jersey and Guernsey besides a new microwave link.

The States Telephone Department operates five local telephone exchanges; Central, the largest, and West are fully automatic and the others in process of conversion. There is Subscriber Trunk Dialling to Britain and direct lines to the United States are planned to meet the needs of merchant banks and other finance activities on the island.

THE PRESS

Jersey's first newspaper, the *Gazette de l'Ile de Jersey*, appeared from 1786 to 1836; during that period a number of other papers, also in French, were published: *Le Chronique*, *Le Constitutionel*, *l'Impartial*, *Le Jersiais*, *Le Miroir* and *La Patrie*, as well as about ten to supply the growing demands of English-speaking readers. Most of these publications, in English or French, reflected the political partisanship of the times and were vitriolic in their attacks on one another. Thus, to a Magot paper, every thief and vagabond was a 'notorious Charlot'. The editor of the *Jersey Times* writes of the editor of the *Constitutionel* as 'a spavined, glandered, broken-down, broken winded, bedevilled, old petti-foggers hack'. The editor of the *British Press* is described by another generous contemporary as a 'mercenary libeller and shuffling coward' whom 'even the fellow Payn, his proprietor, stupid and contemptible as he is, must loathe'. One wonders how they managed to live together on one small island.

Over the following years many magazines, reviews and satires flashed across the local firmament, but by the beginning of World War II the established local press consisted of *The Jersey Morning News* and *The Jersey Evening Post*. In 1940, the proprietors of the *Morning News* decided to close down their paper and destroy their equipment rather than serve the German occupiers. The *Evening Post*, on the other hand, felt that to give the island some sort of information service must be paramount and continued to publish as long as it was able—which meant, with certain interruptions, right through the war. German censors and propaganda writers were installed in its offices and the newspaper was much criticised for its 'collaboration'—which would certainly have resulted in its peremptory closure in any other occupied country. Some passive resistance was, however, continued by its staff, hilarious misprints appearing in the German-inspired sections and bringing some joy in those depressing times.

After the war an effort was made to revive the *Morning News*, but the difficulty of distributing a newspaper all over the island early in the morning proved insurmountable and it closed. The *Evening Post* has since had the field to itself; it gives a wide and thorough coverage of local events, an excellent news service and has supported many causes and new ideas. Though it comes in for its share of criticism, the paper's pungent editorials have done much to shape and guide public opinion in island affairs.

TELEVISION AND RADIO

Channel Television, the Independent TV station set up expressly to serve the islands, started transmitting in September 1962. It is a tribute to the regard in which it now stands that when it ran into financial trouble during the winter of 1973–4 there were offers of help from all quarters—including one lady who volunteered to organise charitable events on its behalf.

The station, which is the smallest in Europe, provides viewers with ITV network programmes as well as original presentations of local and topical interest—even, on occasion, drama in Jersey-French—and very full news coverage. The island's offerings have been highly praised by British critics, who have visited Jersey from time to time, and commended in international competitions.

Television programmes are also received from the BBC and from France, although BBC 2 is not so far available and colour still has to be brought to the island. There is considerable criticism of the BBC's service to the island, which includes scanty regional coverage, and the view has been canvassed that the States might levy its own broadcasting licences instead of, as now, paying these to the BBC to the tune of something approaching £1 million.

A special committee of the States is investigating the whole question of radio and television broadcasting in Jersey. Several contenders have been seeking the franchise to operate a local radio station, among them Channel Television, which sees it as a logical extension to its other services, and the *Evening Post*. At present the matter remains in abeyance.

EDUCATION

Education in the island has a very long history. As early as 1477, the grammar school of St Mannelier was founded through the gifts of Jean Hue, rector of St Saviour, and of Vincent Tehy, who also founded a second grammar school, St Anastase. These existed until the 1840s, when they were incorporated into Victoria College, Jersey, the public school in which Queen Victoria took a considerable personal interest. The Huguenots encouraged education as a counter to superstition and compulsory public education was introduced into the island well in advance of its start in Britain.

Today the States Committee of Education is responsible for twenty-seven primary and six secondary schools. These include Victoria College, which has boarding facilities, and Jersey College for Girls—a public school with historical links with Cheltenham Ladies College and Brighton and Hove High School for Girls. There is also a co-educational grammar school and all three offer courses leading to university entrance or to other forms of higher education. There are plans to introduce more comprehensive schools and the possibility that Victoria College will be turned into a sixth-form co-educational college. A number of other schools are privately run, some by religious bodies or educational trusts. Various ancillary services include a schools' dental clinic, a domestic science centre, a remedial unit, a junior training centre and educational psychology services.

Charles I, at the instance of Archbishop Laud, founded fellowships in 1635 at Exeter, Jesus and Pembroke Colleges, Oxford, for natives of Jersey and Guernsey. These have since been increased by various benefactions, but in general the States Education Committee operates a system of grants for advanced education in Britain on scales similar to the British ones.

The committee also provides a College of Further Education. This offers day-release courses in technical subjects for those in employment, as well as a wide range of adult evening vocational, cultural and recreational courses. At Highlands College there are full-time courses leading to national qualifications in nursery nursing, catering and business studies. For agricultural and horticultural students already employed in the industry, courses are held at the Howard Davis Farm, Trinity.

Education expenditure works out at approximately £300 per pupil, compared with £212 in 1961.

Library services

The libraries are the responsibility of the local authority education committees. The central library, the Bibliothèque Publique, was founded in 1736 on the gifts of Philippe Falle, dean and Jersey historian; there is also a branch library in the west of the island, a junior section, and a mobile library which visits schools and serves outlying areas.

HOUSING

Jersey's housing problems since the war have been formidable. The States Housing Committee has introduced strict laws to govern lettings; large-scale housing projects have been carried out by both States and private endeavour, and vast sums of money advanced to help first-time buyers, yet the deficiency remains. With an estimated population density of some 1,600 people per square mile and the rival demands of agriculture, land has become a precious commodity. Its costs averaged £3,150 per acre or 7p per square foot in 1972. The only way to reduce housing expenditure is by increased density accommodation, such as high rise apartment blocks. Some progress is being made and most of the land required for future development has now been earmarked: this would be sufficient to house an increase in population from the present 72,300 up to 80,000; a further 250 acres would accommodate an additional 10,000 people. It is suggested, perhaps over-optimistically, that the present housing list of some 1,280 families may soon be halved.

While the States opposes subsidies for housing, economic rents are charged for its accommodation and there is a rent rebate system for those in need. In 1971, 2,181 houses were being rented from the States, compared with 1,202 a decade earlier, while 2,232 had been purchased through the system of States loans in comparison with only 160 in 1961. The number of households without a fixed bath, or who had to share, fell from 39 per cent in 1961 to 22 per cent in 1971; the number without a WC, or who had to share, dropped from 26 per cent to 14 per cent in the same period.

WATER SUPPLY

The Jersey New Waterworks Company, founded in 1869, has the task of maintaining an adequate water supply from a necessarily limited reservoir capacity to meet an ever-growing demand; in times of drought severe restrictions have to be imposed. Mains supplies still cover only a quarter of the island. Annual demand in 1961 was 723 million gallons; by 1971 this was up to 1,078, an increase of 50 per cent, and by 1972 it was reaching 1,200 million gal. The five storage reservoirs give a total nominal capacity of 335 million gal. There are besides three or four abstraction points from which water is pumped from springs to the reservoirs. The total catchment area is 8,800 acres, but an average rainfall of 33in is necessary to supply 1,100 million gal of water.

As a means of bridging the gap between demand and supply, a Weir-Westgarth oil-fired distillation plant for de-salination of sea-water was installed at La Rosière, Corbière, in 1968, at a cost of £1·25 million. This multistage flash distillation plant produces an average of 100 million gal a year.

The search for sites for new reservoirs goes on and there is a suggestion that metering of water supplies should be introduced as a means of bringing cost and consumption into a closer relationship with each other. The waterworks company is a private concern, though bound by an Act of the States which sets an upper limit on its charges.

ELECTRICITY

Electricity was late in coming to the island. It was not until 1923 that the Parish of St Helier entered into a contract with a British company for electricity generation and supply for public requirements. In April 1924, the Jersey Electricity Company was registered and the following year started serving 110 consumers, mostly from the business and trading community in the town centre, at a cost of 4p a unit. In 1935, the company began extending supply to the whole island by means of 6·6kV high-tension underground cable and 5·15kV low-tension overground cable. In 1956, the changeover from 6kV to 11kV cable commenced.

The main power station was then at Queen's Road, though there was a smaller one near St Helier Harbour. In the late 1950s it became clear that this was insufficient for an increasing demand, and by 1966 a new power station was built at La Collette, St Helier. In 1968, the first of its three 30mW oil-fired steam turbines was in operation and, by 1973, two others, as well as four 5mW diesels, were transferred from Queen's Road. With a total output of 110mW, the station is still capable of having one further 30mW turbine installed if necessary.

Queen's Road power station is still used as a standby, but is only manned operationally when there are difficulties at La Collette. Plant there comprises approximately 18mW of diesel plant and one 17·5mW Olympus gas turbine, commissioned in December 1973.

Electrical generation faces the problem of oil costs; during 1973, these trebled from £843,000 to £2·5 million. In the first quarter of 1974 the price of electricity went up by 70 per cent, while the offpeak heating tariff rose by nearly 100 per cent.

Urgent studies are now going on into finding ways of producing electricity more economically. One possibility is that of converting the energy obtained from burning refuse, which could result in a saving of about 700,000gal of oil a year.

The States had acquired the whole of the issued Ordinary Share Capital of the JEC in 1936 and so secured control of it, on voting power, though there were other classes of shares still in private hands. In this way ownership is shared between public and private sectors, and of the eight directors on its board, four represent the States. The company is self-financing and does not receive any kind of States assistance.

GAS

Increased demand for gas supplies since World War II has involved the Jersey Gas Light Company in large capital investment. A new retort house installation was commissioned in the mid-1950s, but the island switched from coal gas to butane oil in 1967–8 as a more economical method of gas production.

The price of butane oil, in line with all oil products, has since risen considerably, however—by 17 per cent in 1973 and another 50 per cent early in 1974; these costs must inevitably be reflected in the charges made to the consumer. Alternative methods of production are being considered with some urgency. Britain's conversion to natural gas means that town gas appliances will cease to be obtainable for Jersey's consumers, and if the island converts to natural gas this will have to be done quickly while conversion kits and trained labour are still available.

REFUSE AND SEWAGE DISPOSAL

Waste disposal presents a perpetual difficulty. A rise of 45 per cent in the amount of refuse between 1963 and 1972 means that tips are filling at an unprecedented rate, while incineration and other disposal or treatment plant are proving inadequate for the demands placed on them.

To meet the need for more tipping space, refuse is being used to reclaim land at La Collette, near St Helier Harbour; the contract for this work, worth several million pounds, has been placed with a Dutch firm of specialists. The reclamation scheme will provide space for storage tanks and a berth for oil tankers supplying the nearby power station; it is also planned to incorporate a yacht marina to relieve the shortage of moorings in the island's harbours, while an area in the centre will remain to be filled and then built upon. This is an expensive project, but one that is considered justifiable when land is already at a premium.

The States Sewerage Board has a plant at Bellozanne, on the north-western outskirts of St Helier, which is a model of its kind and has aroused worldwide interest for its success in reducing pollution and ensuring the economic usage of waste material. Formerly a plant belonging to the parish, it has been

Plate 15 The islanders at work: (*above left*) early planting of seed potatoes; (*above right*) packing up cauliflowers for transportation; (*below*) collecting seaweed – known locally as *vraic* – by horse-drawn cart. Further piles of vraic can be seen in the background. It is widely used as a fertiliser.

Plate 16 Farmhouses: (*above*) a typical Jersey farmhouse, built in granite. Note the granite basin in front of the pump. The hydrangea in the foreground grows in such profusion in the island as almost to be a weed; (*below*) a farm near Rozel. The root crops hanging upside-down are Jersey swedes being dried for seed. Other plants including cabbages are treated in the same manner

enlarged, modernised and re-equipped to keep abreast of demand, and in 1959 a biologically activated sludge plant was added to treat sewage. Originally designed to meet the needs of a population of 60,000, it has been extended to treat the sewage of 125,000 and can be further enlarged to cope with 175,000. This plant has made it possible to cease all pumping of effluent into the sea, so that the island's waters are exceptionally clean. The treated sludge is sold to farmers as fertiliser and the methane produced in the processing is used to generate enough electricity to run the plant.

For refuse disposal there are two incinerators and a composting plant. It is planned, however, to phase out the composting plant and replace all other plant by a single, big incinerator. It is proposed that energy recovered from this should be used either for electricity generation or partly for this and partly for heating two of the island's hospitals. Ferrous metals, waste paper and board are all recycled at the plant and consideration is being given to the possibility of recycling glass and tyres.

THE POLICE

A small uniformed police force was introduced in the nineteenth century, when its jurisdiction did not extend beyond St Helier. Though still technically subservient to the centeniers —the honorary police—the force has gradually expanded over the years and its powers have increased in very real ways. From being little more than town beadles bearing the disparaging title of 'paid police', the States Police have become a fully organised and dedicated body, 130 strong, including women officers, under the control of a chief officer.

FIRE SERVICE

The fifty-four men of the States Fire Service include some

civilians who operate its radio control equipment. Despite the many old buildings, serious fires are a rarity—a tribute to the fire prevention measures taken by the service. There were, for instance, no major fires in 1973 and only six which were categorised as medium. Nevertheless, in parallel with population rises, the number of calls received increased from 1,189 in 1969 to 1,460 in 1973.

The service is equipped with two Dennis pump escape appliances, with 50ft and 55ft escapes; a Magirus 81ft ladder on a Bedford chassis; two Dennis water tenders; and, in addition— as mains water is not available all over the island—a 1,200gal water-carrier, also on a Bedford chassis. It also possesses two Zodiac inflatable inshore rescue craft which are transported by road to wherever they are needed, and it operates a cliff rescue service; over the years these have saved many lives.

The States Police and the States Fire Service both come under the control of the Island Defence Committee and share accommodation in St Helier in what was formerly the town arsenal of the militia in Rouge Bouillon.

SOCIAL SERVICES

From earliest times the people in the island's close-knit community received help of all kinds from the parish assemblies, and in the eighteenth century this was extended when a hospital, an infirmary, an orphanage and a workhouse were provided by various private benefactors.

Today, the States Social Security Department provides sickness, accident, maternity and widows' benefits; guardians' allowances for those in charge of orphans; death grants, and an income-related family allowance, paid from the first child. There is a contributory pension scheme—in cases of need a non-contributory pension is available—and a health insurance scheme. The department acts as agent for the payment of

British War Pensions and operates a labour exchange, 'The Jobcentre'. Various supplementary welfare grants are made by the parish authorities as a continuation of their traditional welfare role, and there is a back-up of over thirty charitable organisations of one sort or another, many of which receive States' assistance.

Contributions are earnings-related, but anyone unable, because of a low level of earnings, to contribute sufficiently so as to provide an adequate return will have his payments made up out of public funds. These are from the general revenues of the States so that there is no question of any penny-pinching being necessary to make the scheme self-financing. Instead of the government paying out at a higher level, it is the contributions which are supplemented.

The employee has to pay 4 per cent of his income into the scheme, while the employer pays $5\frac{1}{2}$ per cent, $1\frac{1}{2}$ per cent of this total going into the health scheme. The self-employed are given the choice between contributing at the highest employer-employee rate or paying 8 per cent of declared income and claiming supplementation like lower-paid workers.

HEALTH SERVICES

Under the Health Insurance Scheme, which forms part of the overall social security scheme, the insured man receives back as a cash benefit about 50 per cent of the payment he has made to a doctor for attention for himself or his family. There is also a pharmaceutical benefit whereby drugs and medicines on an approved list are available on payment of a nominal sum. Dental treatment is not covered, but is available free to those in need.

Treatment at the island's well-equipped General Hospital is free, and there are a number of more or less specialist hospitals which provide their services according to a graduated scale and, where necessary, without charge.

The Public Health Committee is responsible for the Medical Officer of Health's Department, for ambulance services and hospitals. Among matters of concern in public health is the high incidence of lung cancer in the island—a result, it is suggested, of cheap tobacco—accounting for 22 per cent of deaths a year.

There is also considerable anxiety that rabies, now rife in Western Europe, may come into the island. To combat this, the penalties for animal smuggling have been increased to £500 or a year's imprisonment for the first offence and £1,000 or two years' imprisonment for the second.

OTHER SERVICES

The island has a customs and excise department—the Impôt; an immigration and nationality department; a weights and measures inspectorate; a public analyst, who is also responsible for much police laboratory work, and a locally run probation service.

9   VISITING JERSEY

JERSEY draws something like a million visitors a year from all over the world, a fact that attests to its numerous attractions. Certainly the scenery is enormously varied, rarely less than enchanting and at times breathtakingly dramatic. With 45 miles of coastline broken into scores of bays and coves, it is possible to find quiet spots away from the holiday crowds even at the height of the season. The beaches are mostly sandy, the sea transparently blue and it is often warm enough to bathe from March right through to October. There is much to recommend a spring or autumn holiday, and some visitors prefer the winter months.

HOTELS AND RESTAURANTS

At every level of accommodation, from smallest guest house to luxury hotel, standards are scrupulously maintained in accordance with the States system of registration. Full details are to be found in the brochure *Invitation to Jersey*, published by the Jersey Hotel and Guest House Association and distributed through the States Committee of Tourism, Weighbridge, St Helier, Jersey.

Service is good and every effort is made to welcome guests and ensure their comfort. By comparison, hotel food is a little disappointing; though of good quality, sufficient quantity and well served, it rarely displays any continental flair. At the bigger hotels there is usually a somewhat uninspired international cuisine, while the smaller establishments provide

149

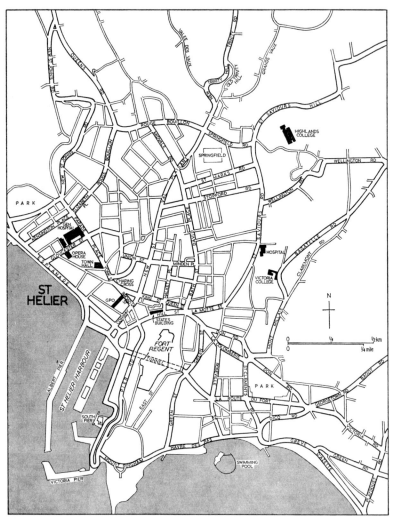

Street plan of St Helier

wholesome if prosaic fare—which is, the hoteliers claim, what their clientele prefer.

There are, however, a number of excellent restaurants of all types and in various parts of the island; these are best discovered by on-the-spot inquiry. Locally caught lobster, crab, crayfish, spider crab, prawns and shrimps are all much sought after, while island-bred pork is excellent and Jersey milk and cream are justly renowned.

Island dishes

Typical local dishes rank more as curiosities than as pleasures for the gourmet. The most appetising is the Jersey bean jar: a pig's trotter cooked with beans for many hours in an earthenware jar or casserole. Transported to the east coast of America, this was said to have provided the inspiration for canned baked beans, though the present-day variety bear little resemblance to a well-seasoned bean jar.

Among the most popular with the local people are dishes prepared from the ormer, or *oreille-de-mer*. These shellfish are sometimes casseroled with pork or bacon and sometimes, after due preparation to make them tender, fried. After the consumption of their contents, the ear-shaped shells of the ormer, with their iridescent mother-of-pearl interiors, often survive as ashtrays.

The traditional 'black butter' is now rarely encountered; it takes about eighteen hours to prepare, hence the 'black butter nights' when stories were told to while away the time. It is made from apples and cider, cooked and stirred over a fire until the apples have become a dark brown pulp; when cool, this is spread on bread. Frankly, after tasting it, one doubts whether the loss of sleep was worth it.

'Jersey wonders' are small, dry, greasy cakes, made by dropping an intricately knotted lump of mix in deep fat. They are sold by bakers, and can best be described as an acquired taste.

PLACES OF INTEREST

St Helier

The residential parts of the island's capital have one or two interesting houses with pretty frontages, dating from late Regency and Victorian times and built by the early British settlers. The main shopping area is concentrated around Queen Street, King Street, Halkett Place and Broad Street. At the centre of the town is Royal Square, a chestnut-lined *place*, where are to be found the offices of the Chamber of Commerce, the States Chamber, the offices of the Bailiff and Crown Officers, the Royal Court and Bibliothèque Publique. When the Royal Court or the States is in session, the proceedings may be witnessed from the public galleries.

The Bibliothèque is also open to the public; the gracious and imposing room housing Philippe Falle's bequest is more reminiscent of a château library than a public institution and, though the need to accommodate more and more books has obscured the room's finer points, the huge fireplace can still be seen, with its picture of Falle above it, and there is a gallery and a dome of some interest.

To the west of the square is St Helier Church, the oldest building in the town, probably begun about the tenth century. It has an austere but impressive interior of rough local granite and its walls are hung with memorials to famous Jerseymen.

A stone's throw away, in Halkett Place, are the public markets, where amid the splendours of Victorian cast iron are stalls offering fruit and vegetables, eggs, bread, meat and French charcuterie. The centrepiece is a fountain, also in wrought iron and extravagantly coloured.

The town hall, in York Street, is a functional corner building built in 1871, whose drab interior has recently been brightened by redecoration and fine displays of flowers in its entrance. The town hall houses the police court and municipal offices;

and the Constable of St Helier has a room there, somewhat like a mayor's parlour in England. On the first floor is an enormous hall used for public meetings and functions; there are a number of fine paintings including 'The Ironing Girl', by David, the French Revolutionary painter.

In Broad Street a strange obelisk commemorates the constableship of Philip Le Sueur, but any dignity it may once have possessed has been diminished by the installation of public lavatories behind it. The island's cenotaph is in Parade Gardens, where there is a large, spreading but uninspiring monument to General Don, the lieutenant-governor responsible, among other things, for much local road-building.

Fort Regent

Now a leisure centre, the fort can be reached by cable car from Snow Hill in the centre of St Helier or by road. It contains a heated swimming-pool, with a separate children's play-pool, a solarium, squash courts and table-tennis rooms, an 18-hole hazard golf course, walks and a children's playground, restaurants, a militia museum and other diversions.

The whole complex is beautifully laid out and the stark military lines of the fort are softened by gardens, vistas, fountains and miniature waterfalls.

Société Jersiaise

The road to Fort Regent passes a fine old Jersey house, the headquarters and museum of the Société Jersiaise, founded in 1873. The fifteen rooms cover all aspects of local life from Palaeolithic to the present day, with sections devoted to geology, archaeology, history, natural history, marine biology, shipping and agriculture. Two of the most interesting exhibits are the St Helier Room and the Jersey Kitchen. Among the museum treasures are a Jersey gold torque dating from 1000 BC; a collection of Armorican coin of 55 BC; the seal used by Charles II

K

153

during the interregnum, and a display of eighteenth-century Jersey silver. The society possesses the largest single library of books on Jersey as well as numerous manuscripts, diaries, historical documents, photographs and old maps; the library is open to scholars and students.

Also housed in the museum is the Barreau Art Gallery, set up in 1928 in memory of Arthur Hamptonne Barreau. It contains a large collection of works of Jersey interest, many by local artists such as Monamy, Philip Jean, P. J. Ouless and the pre-Raphaelite, Sir John Millais, who was a Jerseyman, as well as a number of the island's modern artists, including their doyen, the late Edmund Blampied.

The Société Jersiaise has done much to conserve local beauty spots and places of historic interest; it has helped with the restoration work at Elizabeth Castle and Mont Orgueil, and was responsible for excavations at La Cotte de St Brelade, which yielded relics of Neanderthal man at least 50,000 years old, and at La Hougue Bie, where perhaps the finest prehistoric tomb in western Europe was revealed in 1924. It also looks after most of the island's numerous dolmens and Neolithic sites.

La Hougue Bie

Of the seven menhirs and eight dolmens remaining in the island, the most interesting is to be found at La Hougue Bie. This 18oft high barrow is surmounted by two medieval chapels, one believed to have been dedicated, by his wife, to the murdered Paysnel, Seigneur de Hambye. During the excavations, the tomb, cruciform in shape, was found at the end of a narrow passage, built from enormous slabs of stone. Inside were the bodies of at least eight people, two of them women. The barrow has a particularly potent atmosphere, which is intensified by a fringe of high, dark trees.

Also at La Hougue Bie is the Société Jersiaise's agricultural museum, where there are ploughs, old Jersey measures, cider presses, a dray, a threshing machine and a traditional hay cart.

One of the island's three Occupation museums is housed in a bunker, built by the Germans during the war, under the lawns edging the barrow; the others are in St Peter's Valley, west of St Helier: one in the German Underground Hospital and the third in another bunker.

Churches

All the twelve parish churches are worth visiting, St Martin's and St Brelade's particularly so. St Martin's is the oldest place of worship in Jersey; it was already spoken of as 'St Martin the Old' when William of Normandy, not yet the conqueror of England, acquired the Channel Islands. At one time it had a *Perquage*, or sanctuary path, down which criminals who had taken refuge in the church could reach the sea and freedom. St Brelade's Church, at the western end of one of the island's most popular bathing beaches, has a small chantry attached to it, now usually called the Fishermen's Chapel.

Of a totally different era—the early 1930s—is the church of St Matthews at Millbrook, the so-called 'Glass Church'. Decorated and furnished entirely in glass designed by the French artist, René Lalique, the work was commissioned in memory of Lord Trent, the former Jesse Boot, founder of Boots the Chemist, by his widow.

Castles

Two of the five castles which helped to defend Jersey through its turbulent history—Mont Orgueil and Elizabeth Castle—remain intact, while the ruins of a third can be seen at Grosnez. A small fort off the foreshore at the west end of St Aubin's Bay is not open to the public.

Mont Orgueil, begun in the twelfth century, is both beautiful and fascinating. It stands on a height dominating the picturesque harbour of Gorey, lined with what were once fishermen's cottages and now mostly hotels and restaurants. The fortress is a particularly impressive example of defensive architecture and it is immediately obvious how impregnable it would be to attacks from land or sea. There were once two moats; if the first was carried by attackers, it was still necessary for them to negotiate the second at the end of a narrow ravine-like path along which men or horses would have had to pass in single file, while being bombarded from the machicolations above. This principle of breaking down the enemy formations is continued within, and stone walls and narrow gates pierced for archers would have enabled quite a small defensive force to hold out against superior numbers.

In the Seymour Tower, the last major addition apart from a watch tower added by the Germans, there are tableaux and a small exhibition of old weapons and other military items. During the summer the castle is floodlit at night, its bleached form standing against the dark sky and the lights along the harbour wall reflected in the water.

Elizabeth Castle, about a mile out in St Aubin's Bay off St Helier, can be reached on foot when the tide is low and at other times by amphibious DUKW. Built in Elizabethan times, it was from here that Sir George de Carteret defied Parliament and proclaimed Charles II as King of England. A tableau in one of the rooms commemorates the royal gift of land in North America which came to be called New Jersey. In many ways Elizabeth Castle is little more than a military post, bleak and austere, but its former barracks house a picture gallery and a Jersey Room containing the golden pistol once owned by Lily Langtry, the famous actress known as the 'Jersey Lily'. Along a causeway to the south is the so-called Hermitage Rock, on the top of which a stone hut was said to have been the cell of the apocryphal St Helier, martyred by sea-rovers. Elizabeth Castle is also floodlit at night.

Grosnez, at the edge of a heath-covered headland in the north of the island, is now no more than a few collapsing walls, a dried moat and a flight of broken steps, the whole presenting the sort of vista of romantic decay so much admired in the early nineteenth century. It has been the inspiration of more than one painting and Victorian engravings showing it by moonlight are to be found in some old Jersey homes. The excuse for visiting it is to admire the magnificent panorama of foaming sea at the foot of towering cliffs, with black-headed gulls wheeling far below. On a clear day it is possible to see from it not only Sark, but also the Guernsey coast.

Manor houses

In many cases dating back to the eleventh century, the island's manor houses have for the most part undergone such restoration and, in some cases even, demolition and rebuilding, as no longer to be considered Norman buildings. All are in private hands, and St Ouen's Manor is still owned by the de Carterets. Some are open to the public on certain days and their fine grounds are worth visiting.

Zoological Park

In the landscaped gardens of Les Augrès Manor is the Jersey Zoological Park, where the collection of animals, tropical birds and reptiles was founded by the world-famous writer, traveller and zoologist, Gerald Durrell, who takes an active, personal interest in it. The Jersey Wildlife Preservation Trust has its headquarters here; it provides a sanctuary for threatened species from all over the world, thus fulfilling a lifelong ambition of its founder. The trust has a membership of 9,000; in addition to income from the zoo, and from subscriptions and gifts, it receives a grant of £1,000 a year from the Jersey States.

Local crafts

At St Ouen, l'Etacq Woodcrafts show wood carvers at work and, almost at the extreme opposite end of the island, at the Jersey Potteries in Gorey village, visitors can see all stages of pottery making; there is also a large shop, and a café where tables are set out in the beautiful gardens.

EXCURSIONS

Excursions can be made by air or sea to Guernsey, Sark, Alderney and, via Guernsey, to the enchanted small island of Herm. There are also trips, taking a day or longer, to St Malo, Dinard, St Brieuc, Mont St Michel, Granville and Carteret. Passports are, in most cases, not required, but special identity cards are obtainable free of charge through the Jersey travel agencies, where all details of such excursions are supplied.

ANNUAL EVENTS

There is an almost continuous summer-long programme of activities of every kind, from fêtes and gymkhanas to regattas and sand racing, and a Spring Festival of miscellaneous events backed by the States Tourism Committee.

Battle of Flowers

The principal attraction is the yearly offering of the Jersey Battle of Flowers' Association, which it has organised, with only a wartime break, since 1902. The Battle of Flowers takes place at the height of the summer tourist season and is unlike any other floral carnival in the world. Each of the numerous floats, some as much as 40ft long, represents a theme carried out in flowers of appropriate form and colour, which must entirely cover the float. The 'battle' in which the magnificent

158

exhibits were torn to pieces has now been abandoned; instead the culmination of the afternoon's display is an aerial bombardment of the crowds by RAF aircraft dropping thousands of flower petals.

The entrants are responsible not only for designing, building and decorating the floats, but also for providing the flowers, which often means actually growing them. It is almost a year-long activity to prepare an entry for the parade and the actual covering of the float with flowers to a specific design takes the whole night, often only just being completed as the programme begins. There are classes of all kinds, including one for wild flowers, always well supported and received. Year after year the number of entries increases, as do their size and intricacy of arrangement; even the busy and overworked nurses of the General Hospital find time to enter for it.

International air rally

The Channel Island Aero Club holds its three-day air rally in the spring, which draws a large international entry; in 1973, 109 aircraft participated. Its well-appointed club at Jersey Airport provides flying instruction at reasonable rates and has a large and enthusiastic membership. Visiting members of recognised British or foreign flying clubs are offered clubroom facilities and parking space at the airport.

National hill climb

The Jersey Motor Cycle and Light Car Club sponsors the National Hill Climb Championship, held at Bouley Bay in July, which attracts many of Britain's leading drivers. The club organises thirty-five events, including a number of hill climbs, rallies, trials and scrambles, as well as a sand-race meeting for both cars and motorcycles at St Ouen's Bay, which always draws large crowds.

RECREATIONAL ACTIVITIES

The Royal Channel Islands Yacht Club, founded in 1862, is internationally famous and has some 900 members. Its facilities are offered to visiting members of recognised clubs, though there is an acute shortage of mooring space at all Jersey harbours; in 1973 St Helier alone provided moorings for nearly 3,000 visiting yachts in addition to local craft. Yachts must clear either St Helier or Gorey; vessels of moderate draught may enter St Aubin's harbour or lie off Belcroute Bay in about 12ft of water. The club's affiliates include a number of island yachting, sailing and racing clubs, and various regattas are held.

There are also clubs devoted to swimming, body-board surfing and skin-diving, and at least three angling and fishing clubs.

Football

The Jersey Football Association has fifteen clubs in its senior league and twenty-three in its Saturday Football League. The Jersey Soccer League has some thirty clubs in its four divisions, including Italian and Portuguese clubs, and there is one in each parish.

The most important event of the local soccer season is the annual inter-island cup final for the Muratti Vase which normally becomes a contest between Jersey and Guernsey. Since 1960 the island has entered a team for the Commonwealth Games and, taking into consideration its size and the limited training facilities available, has done extremely well.

Miscellaneous sports

The island's eighteen rifle clubs are a reminder of the days when such activities were supported by the militia. There are also clubs covering netball, tennis, badminton, squash racquets, cricket, golf, rugby football, boxing, archery, cycling, athletics, bowls, drag hunting, go-karting, rock-climbing, roller-skating, tug-o'-war, and billiards and snooker—a very popular local game.

CULTURAL SOCIETIES

L'Assembliée d'Jerriais, founded in 1951, seeks to preserve the Norman-French patois; it sponsors entries in the local music and drama festival, holds whist drives, discussions and debates, an annual service and a Christmas service of nine lessons and carols, and a yearly dinner. The society has about 500 members and at all of its activities Jersey-French is used.

The high standard of acting and the considerable literary gifts to be found among its members have been recognised outside Jersey: George Le Feuvre, who writes a Jersey-French column in the *Evening Post*, recently received an award of merit in a major French literary contest, and Frank Le Maitre, who produced the first French-Jersiais dictionary, was made a Doctor of Letters of the University of Caen and a Fellow of the Royal Academy of the University of Uppsala.

The assembliée's biannual bulletin is sent to universities and libraries all over the world. Evening classes in the patois, run by the society at the Jersey College of Further Education, have attracted a wide following not confined to those born in Jersey.

Other societies

There is a film society, a society of artists, also camera clubs and about nine musical groups, including the Band of the Island of Jersey, another relic of militia days. Of the three amateur dramatic societies, the Jersey Green Room Club, founded in 1909, is the largest and best known; its annual pantomimes are among the island's most popular events.

Community life is particularly lively in Jersey: nearly 300

local societies of all kinds are listed in the *Evening Post Almanac*, in addition to nineteen agricultural and horticultural societies, fifty-seven charitable bodies and district nursing associations. One purely local organisation is the Love Apple League, taking its title from a synonym of the tomato. This is a children's society with branches at most schools; its activities include the collection of funds for hospitals 'adopted' by a particular branch, among them children's hospitals all over Britain.

BIBLIOGRAPHY

ARTHUR, JEAN and STEVENS, JOAN. 'Archives', *Bulletin of the Société
Jersiaise*, vol 21, part 1, 25–32, 1973
BALLEINE, G. R. *The Bailiwick of Jersey*, 1951
——. *A History of the Island of Jersey*, 1950
CARMAN, W. Y., FSA, FR HIST S. 'Jersey Militia Colours', *Bulletin of
the Société Jersiaise*, vol 20, part 3, 302–6, 1971
DE GRUCHY, MAJOR F. A. L. 'The Royal Jersey Militia and the
Military Role of Jersey in History', *Bulletin of the Société Jersiaise*,
vol 16, part 4, 365–72, 1956
FENWICK, R. G. *Abridged Report by R. G. Fenwick, HM Inspector of
Constabulary, of the Inspection of the States of Jersey Police Force*, States
of Jersey, 1971
GREFFE, JERSEY STATES. *Act, dated 12 November 1970, and Report of the
Committee of Agriculture regarding future agricultural policy, together
with a Proposition relative thereto*, Jersey States, 1970
——. *Amendments to the Report and Proposition of the Committee of Agri-
culture regarding future agricultural policy*, Jersey States, 1971
——. *Report and Proposition regarding the Scale and Pattern of Develop-
ment in the Island over the next five years*, Jersey States, 1974
LEMPRIÈRE, RAOUL. *Portrait of the Channel Islands*, 1970
MAUGHAM, R. C. F. *The Island of Jersey Today*, 1938; revised 1950
MOLLET, RALPH. 'Military Colours of the Royal Militia Island of
Jersey', *Bulletin of the Société Jersiaise*, vol 17, part 4, 337–8, 1960
POWELL, G. C. *Economic Survey of Jersey*, States of Jersey, 1971
STATES DEPARTMENT OF AGRICULTURE. *Statistics, 1973*, States of
Jersey, 1974
STEVENS, JOAN. 'A Review of the Past Century', *Bulletin of the Société
Jersiaise*, vol 21, part 1, 6–16, 1973
UTTLEY, JOHN. *The Story of the Channel Islands*, 1966
VATCHER, COLONEL H. M., MC. 'The Royal Militia Island of Jersey,
1939–45', *Bulletin of the Société Jersiaise*, vol 15, part 3, 317–28, 1951
WOOD, ALAN and MARY. *Islands in Danger*, 1955

ACKNOWLEDGEMENTS

HERE I would like to record my gratitude to all who have helped me: Miss Ruth Amy, honorary secretary of the Assembliée d'Jerriais; Mr M. A. F. Bartley, chief engineer, States' Sewerage Board; Mr Alan Le Brun, chief immigration officer, Immigration and Nationality Department; Mr Rodney Clark, engineer manager, Jersey New Waterworks Co Ltd; Mrs Ellaine Le Cornu, general secretary, Jersey Motor Cycle and Light Car Club; Mr John Hartley, secretary, Jersey Wildlife Preservation Trust; Mrs E. Hyland, personal assistant to the secretary, Jersey Battle of Flowers Association; Mr J. H. Lees, controller, States Social Security Department; Mr W. G. Mahoney, chief fire officer, States Fire Service; Mr D. Mannion, secretary, Royal Jersey Agricultural and Horticultural Society; Mrs Dorothy Minns, secretary, Jersey Hotel and Guest House Association; Mr L. A. Minty, secretary, Jersey Farmers' Union; Mr G. I. G. Pitman, chief administrative officer, States Department of Public Building and Works; Mr Leslie Rebindaine, chief executive officer, States Department of Tourism; Mrs Joan Stevens, president, the Société Jersiaise.

Especially I would like to express my gratitude and appreciation to those old friends who went to so much trouble to help me: Senator Clarence Farley, John Abraham, Roy Mourant, Bob Baker and Edward Owen.

ACKNOWLEDGEMENTS

I am grateful to those listed below for permission to use their photographs in my book:

British Tourist Authority: 1 (above), 2 (above, left), 3 (below), 4, 5 (above), 7, 11, 12, 14, 15 (below), and 16
J. Allan Cash: 2 (below)
Phillip E. Coffey: 13 (above)
Jersey Evening Post: 15 (above, left and right)
States of Jersey Tourism Committee: 1 (below), 2 (above, right), 3 (above), 5 (below), 6, 8, 9 and 10

INDEX

INDEX

168